HOLY WEEK AD 33

LARRY LASTRAPES

GSV
PRESS

HOLY WEEK AD 33

THE PROPHECIES, EVENTS, AND ACTIVITIES BEFORE, DURING, AND AFTER HOLY WEEK

LARRY LASTRAPES

Holy Week - AD 33

This publication is designed to provide accurate and authoritative information in regard to the subject matter covered. It is sold with the understanding that neither the author nor the publisher is engaged in rendering legal, investment, accounting or other professional services.

Disclaimer: *The writer, editor and publisher of this book has attempted to give proper credit to all sources and illustrations used in this text. Any miscredit or lack of credit is unintended and will be credit in the next edition.*

HOLY BIBLE TEXT USED IS FROM THE FOLLOWING:

Douay-Rheims Bible (internet English version)

Douay-Rheims Haydock Commentary – Rev. George Leo Haydock

The Didache Bible – RSV: With commentaries based on the Catechism of the Catholic Church – Ignatius Bible Edition

Ignatius Catholic Study Bible: New Testament - RSV: Second Catholic Edition - Ignatius Press 2010

New American Bible, Revised Edition (NABRE), United States Conference of Catholic Bishops

A Catholic Commentary on Holy Scripture

Thomas Nelson and Sons Publisher 1953

Book Cover: Martin Lastrapes
Cover Artwork: "Triumphal Entry - Maesta" by Duccio Di Buoninsegna

ISBN: 979-8-9892037-0-3

CONTENTS

ABSTRACT

In the late 1990s my Catholic pastor at the time, in one of his sermons, said that the Catholic religion is a continuation of the Jewish religion. After hearing about the ancient Jewish prophecy that the bread and wine offerings will replace animal sacrifices, my pastor's statement came to mind. I realized that, through the fulfillment of that ancient Jewish prophecy, the Catholic religion is, in fact, a continuation of the Jewish Religion. This reinforced my belief that I needed a deeper understanding of the ancient Jewish religion, culture, teachings, and history of the Jews before I could develop a better understanding of my Catholic religion. As I learned more about the Jewish religion, I realized that I needed this knowledge before I could improve my understanding of the Catholic religion more fully.

As I looked at the activities that took place during the week before Jesus was crucified, I realized that I needed to begin by looking at the early history of the Israelites. In the New Testament, it tells us that they knew that the Messiah was coming but I found myself asking, "How did they know that?" Through my research, I discovered that the life and beliefs of the Jewish people revolved around the Old Testament teachings. The prophecies in the Old Testament pointed to the coming of the Messiah and the New Testament documents how those prophecies were fulfilled. There is a saying about the bible that I heard a few decades ago that comes to mind. The saying: "The New Testament is concealed in the Old Testament, and the Old Testament is revealed in the New Testament". This is a basic description of the fundamental difference between the Old Testament and the New Testament. In other words, the Old Testament prophecies tell us about the coming of the Messiah and the New Testament tells us how those Old Testament prophecies were fulfilled by Jesus.

The New Testament also tells us that in the year that Jesus was crucified, He made a public proclamation that He was the long-awaited Messiah and King as He made it known that His arrival was foretold in the Old Testament. This proclamation was made on a Sabbath day during the religious services in the synagogue. He made this proclamation in the final year of his public ministry when He read the following passage from the book of the prophet Isaiah:

> *The spirit of the Lord is upon me because He has anointed me to preach good news to the poor. He has sent me to proclaim release to the captives and recovering of sight to the blind, to set at liberty those who are oppressed, to proclaim the acceptable year of the Lord.*
>
> Isaiah 61:1-2

After Jesus read this passage from the prophet Isaiah, the New Testament goes on to tell us what Jesus did next.

> *And He closed the book, gave it back to the attendant, and sat down; and the eyes of all in the synagogue were fixed on Him. And He began to say to them, "Today this scripture has been fulfilled in your hearing."*
>
> Luke 4:18-21

Additionally, the Old Testament told us how we could recognize the Messiah when he arrived. In the Old Testament book of Zechariah, we are told that the Messiah would arrive in Jerusalem riding on a donkey. During His triumphal entry into Jerusalem, Jesus arrived riding a donkey on the Sunday before He was crucified.

Rejoice greatly, O daughter Zion! Shout aloud, O daughter of Jerusalem! Behold: your king comes to you; triumphant and victorious is he, humble, and riding on a donkey, on a colt, the foal of a donkey.

Zechariah 9:9

Then there was another item of confusion that needed clarification for me. Throughout the Old Testament, we read about the Hebrews, Israelites, and Jews; then in the New Testament, we read about the Christians. For some years, I was confused and did not know the difference between a Hebrew, an Israelite, or a Jew. I finally decided that this confusion had run its course and it was time for me to re-direct my research. I wanted to know why they seemed to be the same people and at the same time, they seemed to be different people.

Who were these groups of people, where did they come from and how did they get their names? Were they the same people or was each group different? This is a piece of my curiosity that needed to be fulfilled. Through my research, I learned that Abraham, a Hebrew, has an interesting history of how and why he was called a Hebrew. My research also revealed to me that the Israelites and the Jews are descendants of Abraham and that in itself is an interesting bit of research that will be explained in more detail later.

Then there are the followers of Jesus who came to be known as Christians. Being a cradle Catholic, it was pretty obvious to me that Christians are those who follow Jesus and believe that He is the Messiah and the Son of God. But, like the Hebrews, Israelites, and Jews, the names Catholic and Christian have an evolutionary history of their own. Over the years I have read the New Testament many times but I never even noticed that the followers of Jesus, after His death and resurrection, did not refer to their religious practice as Catholic nor did they refer to themselves as Christians.

Believe it or not, it was the persecutors of the followers of Jesus who were the first ones to call them Christians. But that name did not define their religious beliefs or practices but rather, that is how the persecutors identified those who were spreading the teachings of Jesus the Christ. The Christians who were being persecuted for spreading the teachings of Jesus referred to their religious practice as "The Way".

In the New Testament Jesus said, *"I am the way, the truth, and the life"* *(John 14:6)*. Recalling those words of Jesus, and His teachings, His followers referred to their religious practice of following the teachings of Jesus as "The Way". Collectively, as a group, the followers of The Way were called the "Church" as noted in the scripture passages below.

> *But this I do admit to you, that according to the <u>Way</u>, which they call a sect...*
>
> Acts 24:14

> *Now there were in the <u>Church</u> at Antioch prophets and teachers.*
>
> Acts 13:1

All of that being said it seems like the followers of Jesus had a real solid identity. But, before long, schisms and religious rivals of the Church were forming, and the Church realized that it needed to distinguish itself from the rival religions. The Church needed to acquire for itself, a different and unique identity. Those who followed the teachings of Jesus had grown in number and they were becoming very widespread. With the Church being so widespread, they needed a name that would identify who they are and depict their geographical status.

There is no known formal documentation on the evolution of the new name for The Way. The earliest known documentation of the formal name for the Church is found in a letter that was written by St. Ignatius of Antioch. It was a farewell letter to his fellow Christians that was written in about AD 108 before he was martyred. In his letter, he referred to the followers of Jesus as The Way and he referred to their Christian religion as the "Catholic Church."

Some 70 years after the death and resurrection of Jesus, His followers had increased in number and their numbers had extended to other countries. Their numbers continued to grow and spread far and wide into the areas that surrounded the Mediterranean Sea and into the known world. With the vastness of the areas covered by the followers of The Way, the new name Catholic seemed to be fitting for their identity. The word catholic is taken from the Greek word *"katholikos"* which means universal.

The followers of The Way began to call themselves the "Catholic Church". Finally, The Way had a new identity that set them apart from other Christians. That worked well for a century or so. But once again, religious identity issues arose as other religions adopted the name Catholic for their religion also. In AD 380 Theodosius I, the emperor of Rome, issued a declaration that limited the use of the term "Catholic Christian" exclusively to those who followed the same faith as the Pope. He declared that Catholic Christianity was the official religion of the Roman Empire. He further declared that the followers of the other religions who called themselves Catholic were heretics.

The declaration of Theodosius I did not stop the other Christian religions from calling themselves Catholic. In the centuries that followed, some Christian religions stopped calling themselves Catholic because they considered the term "Catholic" to be highly insulting. From the 6th century to the 10th century the Christians who followed the Pope were referred to as the "Roman Catholic

Church". Per the Oxford English Dictionary, the title "Roman Catholic Church" has been applied to the whole church in the English language since the Protestant Reformation occurred in the late 16th century.

As I continued my studying of the teachings of the Catholic religion and compared those teachings to the teachings and cultural norms of the Jewish religion, several times I was reminded of that old Jewish prophecy that a bread and wine offering will replace the sacrificing of lambs in the temple. The Old Testament prophecies, cultural traditions, and the teachings of the apostles indicated that the Jewish religion would experience an evolutionary change. That change, as I recalled from Dr. Scott Hahn's writings on the Eucharist, is that an ancient Jewish theologian prophesied that the bloody sacrificing of lambs in the Temple would come to an end and be replaced with a bread and wine offering. As I learned more about this prophetic evolutionary change, as mentioned earlier, I realized that The Catholic religion, with the bread and wine offering that is present in the Catholic Mass, is the fulfillment of that ancient Jewish prophecy.

In Catholicism, we believe that the Bible is the inspired Word of God. The inspired word of God means that we believe that God has spoken to us through the prophets and He has delivered His teachings to us through the Bible. The Bible is God's Word and His law; the entire human race has been instructed by God through the Bible on His laws that govern their lives.

INTRODUCTION

As I learned more and more about the Catholic religion I found myself wanting to share this knowledge with my family, friends, and acquaintances. That has been the driving force that encouraged me to write this document. Now, I want to share it with everyone. As I wrote about the activities that took place during the week before Jesus was crucified I realized that some of those activities could be difficult to understand. I concluded that a basic knowledge of the ancient Jewish religion, culture, traditions, and norms was needed. As I researched and wrote about the background of the Jewish people, this narrative began to develop to the point that it became a learning experience and religious journey for me.

I would like to extend to you, the reader, a personal invitation to join me on this religious journey. I want to share with you the insight that I have gained through the teachings of Christian theologians with a focus on the final week of Our Lord's time here on earth. Sometimes it is difficult and even challenging to comprehend the religious interpretations and teachings of the theologians. One of my objectives in this narrative is to present the theological teachings of the theologians in a format that, hopefully, will make them easier to understand. As much as possible, I will be using the inspired Word of God, the Bible, to validate the writings of the theologians. In addition to using the Bible, some of the religious teachings will also be validated with scientific documents and world events that support those religious teachings.

The coming of the Messiah was prophesied in the Old Testament with the fulfillment of those prophecies documented in the New Testament. Those Old Testament prophecies of the Messiah were fulfilled with the coming of Jesus Christ. My primary focus will be the period of time between Palm Sunday and Easter Sunday, the final week of Jesus' life here on earth. In Christianity, this time period is called Holy Week. During Holy Week, several different messianic prophecies from the Old Testament and religious teachings were being fulfilled on each day of that week. Additionally, the Old Testament prophecies told us several things to help us recognize the Messiah. We are told when he would arrive; where he would arrive; and how he would make his arrival and presence known.

This narrative is based on my personal research, study, and religious journey for the past five (5) decades. My religious research was rather casual over those decades but it does cover a period of about 50 years. It will focus on Jesus, the Messiah, and the historical events that preceded and defined His arrival. Over the years, from time to time, I have had questions about the things that took place during Holy Week and how they were related to the teachings of the Catholic religion. In my research, it has been my objective to answer those nagging questions.

In addition to the events that took place during Holy Week, I learned about the influences that religious and secular leaders have had on each other and how those influences molded and shaped the society that existed during the time of Jesus. That would include some of the cultural and religious norms of the Jewish people that influenced and molded modern-day Christianity.

Other significant events that will be discussed include the norms that shaped Jewish society during the time of Jesus. The Jewish calendar, lambing of the sacrificial lambs (the process of birthing lambs), and their correlation to the birth of Jesus and how they were very important in Jewish society.

Religiously, I have been a Roman Catholic from birth, which, by definition makes me a cradle Catholic. Like me, my parents were cradle Catholics also and they were very strong in their Catholic beliefs and practices. As far back in my childhood as I can remember, I went to church with my parents every Sunday and Catholic Holy days. As I grew older, I continued attending Catholic services but gradually, as the years passed, I began to question the practices and norms of the Catholic religion. The practices and norms that I did not understand were coupled with questions and influences of other non-Catholic religions. Although I questioned some of the teachings of the Catholic religion, I would never leave my religion without knowing and understanding what I would be leaving.

When I was in my twenties, some five decades ago, I decided that I needed to understand the practices and norms of my religion. I needed answers to the many questions that I had about my Catholic religion and, consequently, I embarked on my quest to get myself educated as a Roman Catholic. Gradually I started researching specific questions I had about my religion and the more I learned about Catholicism, the stronger my religious ties grew for the Catholic religion.

Initially, my religious research was limited to the books and documents I had in my possession. In recent years, with the advent of the internet, my research has broadened immensely. By using the internet I was able to proceed with a broadened search for the answers to the many questions that dwelled inside of me. I was able to find books and articles written by religious scholars on numerous subjects. For me and my religious research, the internet was heaven-sent.

One of the many questions I dwelled on for several years was the year that Jesus was crucified. I have always heard, in a variety of religious conversations and different religious media that Jesus died in the year AD 33. As I searched the internet, I discovered that religious scholars did not always agree on the year or the day of the week that Jesus was crucified. Although each of the four gospels in the New Testament (Matthew, Mark, Luke, and John) state that Jesus was crucified on a Friday, some religious scholars believe Jesus was crucified on a different day of the week. Some believe it was a Tuesday while others believe that it could have been on a Wednesday or Thursday but the majority of them agree that the day of the crucifixion was a Friday.

Additionally, many of the same religious scholars who cannot agree on the day of the week that Jesus was crucified, cannot agree on the year that Jesus was crucified either. The years AD 27, AD 30, AD 33, and AD 34 are the most common years that some of them believe Jesus was crucified. As I read through some of the narratives that were written by a few religious scholars, I found myself enveloped in a world of confusion. I am not a religious scholar by any stretch of the imagination but, for my peace of mind, I needed to understand their analogies and test them against the findings of my research that is based on modern-day technology.

As I understand the four Gospel writers in the New Testament, each one of them say that Jesus was crucified on a Friday.

You know that after two days the Passover is coming, and the son of man will be delivered up to be crucified.

Matthew 26:2

And when evening had come since it was the day of preparation, that is, the day before the Sabbath...

Mark 15:42

It was the day of Preparation, and the Sabbath was beginning.

Luke 23:54

Since it was the day of Preparation, to prevent the bodies from remaining on the cross on the Sabbath...

John 19:31

As I read these passages from the bible I cannot help but wonder how these bible translations could be translated as a day different than Friday. To clarify the scripture passages above, the day of preparation is the day before the first day of the Feast of Unleavened Bread. In the year that Jesus was crucified, based on the NRSV (New Revised Standard Version), bible translation used by the Catholic Church, the day of preparation was a Thursday and the first day of the Feast of Unleavened Bread was a Friday. In the Jewish calendar, the beginning of the day was in the evening when three stars were officially visible. Normally, three stars were officially visible at about 6:00 PM. I don't want to get into too much detail at this point but, for clarification, the first day of the Feast of Unleavened Bread, in the year AD 33 in the Jewish calendar, was the sixth day of the week and it was a Sabbath day. In the Jewish calendar and our modern-day calendar, the sixth day of the week is always Friday. If you did not catch what is being said in the last two sentences, it may be worth repeating. Yes, that is correct; the Friday that Jesus was crucified was a Sabbath day. This is another topic that sparked my curiosity and caused me to research it for a better understanding.

To get a different perspective on some of the religious discussions I decided to reach out to the scientific community. I decided to focus on the research of two non-religious scholars as I attempted to understand and learn more about the year that Jesus was crucified. Two Oxford scientific scholars, using modern-day astronomical technology, researched the year of the crucifixion as they went back in time using modern-day technology. Based on the fulfillment of an Old Testament prophecy of a blood moon appearing on the day of the crucifixion, I coupled that prophecy with the research results of the two Oxford scholars and discovered that the scholars were able to scientifically validate the appearance of a blood moon on a Friday in the year AD 33. This may sound pretty simplified but that's when I concluded that Jesus was crucified in the year AD 33. With my newfound confidence that the year AD 33 was accurate, I decided to use that year in the title of this narrative. The details of the results of the two Oxford scholars' research that influenced my choice are discussed in more detail later.

Over the past 50 years, when I was not sure about any particular Catholic teachings, practices, or norms, I would begin researching them in an attempt to find some answers. Initially, I was reading documents that, at times, only added confusion to my doubts and understanding. But I persisted in my research and that persistence had a twofold benefit for me. Gradually, as my research continued, I noticed that my current research was beginning to make some of my earlier research easier to understand. And, as the understanding of my earlier research increased, that newfound understanding was making my ongoing research easier to understand and less confusing as well. I still have a very, very long way to go in my religious knowledge but I have learned a lot about my Catholic religion over the past five decades.

There was a time when I was afraid, very uncomfortable, and reluctant to discuss my religion with Catholics and non-Catholics because my religious knowledge was very limited. As I have already mentioned, I am not a religious scholar by any stretch of the imagination but now, after 50 years of research on various religious teachings, I have more confidence in my religious knowledge and I enjoy discussing the Catholic religion. Whenever I am able, I also enjoy explaining the teachings of the Catholic religion to other Catholics and non-Catholics as well. Of course, my primary focus is on the teachings that I understand. In many instances, those discussions lead to questions that I cannot answer and I follow up by searching for answers to those questions. Now that I have this hunger for religious knowledge it has become very difficult for me to let it rest when I am faced with an unanswered question.

Over the years my religious research has branched out into many different directions. For many years I had an ardent curiosity about the Last Supper. I wanted to know what took place during the Last Supper. About 20 years ago I launched and focused my research on the Last Supper to fulfill my curiosity about the events that took place during the Last Supper. It may be obvious to most people but for me, it was a discovery when I learned that the Last Supper was the Jewish Passover. That was another spark that enflamed my burning desire to learn more about the time period when Jesus walked on this earth.

I am very excited to share the things that I have learned about the Last Supper and how it ties in with the crucifixion and death of Jesus. I have learned, in my more recent research that the year that Jesus died was a jubilee year. That in itself is very significant in the redemptive mission of Jesus.

Each year, during the annual Passover, the population in Jerusalem increased from the norm of about 15,000 to more than 150,000 people. In the year that Jesus was crucified the Jewish people were looking for the messiah and they anticipated his arrival that year because it was a Jubilee Year. Each day during Holy Week the temple area was very crowded and, during those five days before his crucifixion, Jesus remained very visible in the temple area. Making Himself visible during the five days before his crucifixion was, in itself, a fulfillment of another Old Testament prophecy. His visibility each day during that week was very risky as He continued teaching the crowds in the temple area.

Although His words seemed to be casual rhetoric to our modern-day ears, Jesus was teaching and telling the people that the Old Testament prophecies about the coming of the Messiah were being fulfilled through Him. Again, this will be discussed in more detail later.

Politically, the Romans were in power over Israel during the time of Jesus. The people expected the Messiah to be a person who would lead them into battle to conquer the Romans and return the rule of Israel to the Jews. The Old Testament prophecies spoke of a Messiah coming in peace but the people failed to recognize Jesus as that peaceful Messiah because of their errant expectations of a Messiah who would lead them into battle against the Romans.

I wanted to understand why and how the Romans gained so much power over the Jews in their own country. This narrative will highlight how the Romans came into power over the Jews as well as the Jewish religious rules, together with their cultural and traditional practices. Those practices are neatly bundled into the prophetic teachings of the Old Testament. Today, the meanings of those prophetic teachings are revealed to us through the Apostles and followers of Jesus. Many of those revelations came to us through the writings that were collected and compiled by Catholic leaders back in the 4th century. Eventually, those inspired documents that were compiled became the document we call the New Testament.

When I was a teenager my mother told me, "The more you know, the more you know you don't know". 50 years of religious research has taught me that those words were very, very true. Now, I have an inner drive to learn as much as I can. More and more I know how much I don't know and it just makes me anxious to know more.

VOCABULARY

Sometimes, when I am researching different topics, I come across words that I need to understand in different situations or in a different context. In my quest to gain a more detailed and better understanding of the different topics that I will be covering, especially Adam and Eve, original sin, and the resurrection of Our Lord, I came across a few words that I needed to gain a more in-depth understanding of their meanings in a religious and scriptural context. Once I had a better grasp of the keywords that I encountered in my research, it was easier for me to explain the different topics as those terms applied. The words that helped me in my research included the following:

1. **Atonement**

2. **Concupiscence**

3. **Ransom and Redemption**

4. **Repentance**

5. **Resurrection**

6. **Salvation**

1. Atonement: In my research, it seems like every term in the bible is derived from Hebrew, Greek, or Latin. Believe it or not, the theological term atonement has its root origin in the English language. The verb "atone" is formed from the two words "at" and "one". When those two words are squeezed together they make the word "atone". Separated or squeezed together, "at one" or "atone" means to reconcile or "make at one" through the satisfaction of an offense. The Atonement of original sin is the ransom that was paid by Jesus. His death on the cross is the ransom that was paid to reconcile the entire world and made it to be "at one" with God.

2. Concupiscence: I have heard this term used many times in my life but I never really knew the true meaning of it. I knew it had something to do with sin and for that reason, I just assumed that it wasn't good. Over the past several weeks I have read numerous articles on the internet as I searched for a definition but none of them were very helpful for me. They all confirmed my assumption that concupiscence is not good but I was not satisfied with their explanations. Their primary focus defined concupiscence as a strong lustful or sexual desire but, for some reason, I felt that it meant more than that. So, I kept searching and reading different articles on the internet websites.

Then I came across an article on the website "Simply Catholic". The article was written by Monsignor (Msgr.) William J. King. It was a mind-opener for me and it confirmed my feeling that concupiscence had a deeper meaning than a lustful or sexual desire. Msgr. King opened his article with the example of a car that desperately needed a wheel alignment. He noted how the driver had to struggle, constantly, to keep the car from veering off the road. When it comes to sin, it is an ongoing challenge to stay on the right path and not veer off course. With concupiscence, it is a tendency or temptation to veer off course and engage in a sinful deed, any sinful deed. Interestingly the Greek word for sin is *harmartia* which means *to miss the mark* or *veer off course*. Note that neither concupiscence nor our thoughts are sinful in themselves because these are tendencies or temptations to go off course and engage in a sinful deed. Engaging in the deed is the actual sin.

Msgr. King also noted that before their sin, Adam and Eve experienced perfect harmony between their body and soul and with God. They did not have this constant tendency or temptation to veer off course but they always had their free will. When Adam and Eve used their free will to veer off course and sinned, the perfect harmony between their body and soul and with God was ruptured. In addition to being alienated from paradise, their mortality was affected as well. Their entire existence was changed by the mortality-related experiences of pain and illness; as well as suffering, aging, death, and decay being introduced into their lives and the lives of their descendants.

When we experience concupiscence, we are experiencing the disharmony between the body and the soul. Because they are not in harmony, the body wants to engage in sinful deeds but at the same time, the soul wants to cling to the higher things of God. In his letter to the Romans, St. Paul wrote about the tug of war between his body and soul that he was experiencing.

> *So I find it to be a law that when I want to do right, evil lies close at hand. For I delight in the law of God, in my inmost self, but I see in my members another law at war with the law of my mind and making me captive to the law of sin which dwells in my members.*
>
> Romans 7:21-23

Long before St. Paul was experiencing concupiscence, Jesus told us what to expect with concupiscence when He was praying in the garden of Gethsemane and He asked Peter to pray with Him.

> *And He came to the disciples and found them sleeping; and He said to Peter, "So, could you not watch with me one hour?*

Watch and pray that you may not enter into temptation;
the spirit indeed is willing but the flesh is weak."

Matthew 26: 40-41

Sin does not exist in Heaven and no one with any stain of sin can dwell in heaven. Although the hereditary stain of original sin is washed away with baptism, and the stains of our personal sins are forgiven through reconciliation and confession, concupiscence was not washed away with baptism nor is it removed through reconciliation and confession. The perfect harmony between our body and soul as well as the perfect harmony with God will not be experienced again until we get to heaven.

3. Ransom and Redemption: These two terms are defined together because they have the same meaning. Redemption, taken from the Latin word *redempto* which is taken from Hebrew and Greek, is the process of taking man from the bondage of sin to liberation through the merits of Christ. The Hebrew term *"kopher"* and the Greek term *"lytron"* in the Old Testament translation means *a ransom price*. As noted in St. Paul's first letter to the Corinthians:

Do you not know that your body is a temple of the Holy
Spirit within you? You are not your own; you were bought
with a price. So glorify God in your body.

1 Corinthians 6:19-20

This is the price that the redeemer paid for our liberation. It is the reversal of the fall of Adam and Eve.

4. Repentance: With this term, the most common saying that I have heard is, "Repent and be saved". The term Repent or repentance is taken from the Greek words *mentanoeo* for repent or *metanoia* for repentance. Either form of the word means *to change your mind*. When Jesus was preaching the Gospel he said:

...The time is fulfilled, and the kingdom of God is at hand;
repent, and believe in the gospel.

Mark 1:14

He is telling his listeners to change their minds about sin and turn to the teachings of the gospel that he was preaching. To repent means more than just changing your mind. In addition to the Greek terms to repent and repentance, we see that the Hebrew word for repent is *tshuva* which means to return. So when you combine the Greek and the Hebrew words for repenting we find that the scripture passages are telling us to change our minds about sin and return to God's teaching. Taking it one step further, a more complete meaning for repentance is changing your mind about sin, returning to God's teachings, and running away from anything that would keep you from God. In the Old Testament God made it clear when He told the Israelites to repent.

Therefore say to the house of Israel, Thus says the Lord God:
Repent and turn away from your idols, and turn away your
faces from all your abominations.

Ezekiel 14:6

5. Resurrection: Resurrection refers to a dead person rising from death and coming back to life again with the full resumption of their normal physical life activities. It only refers to the physical body coming back to life and not the soul coming back to life because the soul does not die.

6. Salvation: The single most important thing that I learned about this term is that salvation is not a one-time event. The redemption of Christ is an invitation to salvation. Salvation is the process of each one of us accepting or rejecting God's supernatural gifts. When a person says that salvation has come into their life, they are saying that they have decided to live their life in alignment with the will of

God. It means that the Christian way of life is being chosen constantly. Salvation is an ongoing process that never ends.

CHAPTER 1

RELIGIOUS AND SECULAR INFLUENCE

The religious world has often been viewed as being separate from the secular (non-religious) world when, in fact, both worlds have always co-existed. Throughout history, the religious world has had a direct influence on the secular world, and the secular world has had a direct influence on the religious world. This co-existence and mutual influence between the two worlds have radiated and left its mark throughout all of history, even to the present day. If we look at the ancient religious and secular leaders, we can see how the two cultures co-existed and influenced each other throughout all of history.

THE RELIGIOUS LEADERS

When I looked into the history of the leaders of the two different worlds, religious and secular, I decided to turn my focus to the religious leaders first. As I looked at the religious leaders who existed before the time of Jesus, my research took me back to His ancestor Abraham, the first religious leader noted in the Old Testament.

Throughout all of history, God has chosen different people to deliver his messages and teachings to the world. We don't know why or how those messengers were chosen but God appeared to them and communicated with them in many different ways throughout the centuries. One of the first religious leaders chosen by God to be His messenger and leader of the people was a man named Abram.

God appeared to Abram for the first time in his home city of Ur which is located in Mesopotamia. God told him to leave the land of his birth, and journey to the land of Canaan.

> *Terah took his son Abram, and Lot the son of Haran, his grandson, and Sarai his daughter-in-law, his son Abram's wife, and they went forth together from Ur of the Chaldeans to go into the land of Canaan;*
>
> Genesis 11:31

Initially, the passage seems to suggest that God appeared to Terah, the father of Abram and told him to go to the land of Canaan. But we see in the New Testament that St. Stephen, the first Christian martyr, confirmed that God appeared to Abram and not his father Terah.

> *...The God of glory appeared to our father Abraham when he was in Mesopotamia before he lived in Haran, and said to him, "Depart from your land and your kindred and go into the land that I will show you. Then he departed forth from the land of the Chaldeans and lived in Haran. And after his father died, God removed him from there into this land in which you are now living."*
>
> Acts 7:2-4

While Stephen was speaking to the Jewish council before they stoned him, he told them how God appeared to Abram in Ur and told him to journey to the land of Canaan. Abram, his father, and their entire household left Ur and journeyed together until they reached the city of Haran in northern Mesopotamia.

After settling in Haran, Abram's journey to the Land of Canaan came to an end. He remained in Haran for some 60 years until the death of his father, Terah. After the death of his father, God spoke to Abram a second time. He was now 75 years old when God told him to leave his father's household in Haran and continue on his journey to the land of Canaan.

> *Now the Lord said to Abram: "Go from your country and your kindred and your father's house to a land that I will show you."*
>
> Genesis 12:1

Abram obeyed the second calling of God and continued his journey to the Land of Canaan. Note on the map that Haran is east of the Euphrates River. As Abram passed through different settlements on his journey to the land of Canaan, the people would ask him about his origin. He told them that he came from beyond the Euphrates. Through my research, I learned that Abram was an 11th-generation descendant of Noah, but I could not find anything about his race or the language that he spoke. In the common language of the inhabitants along his journey to the land of Canaan, the word hebrew meant "from beyond". He came to be known as Abram "from beyond" or Abram the "Hebrew". And so, over the decades that passed, the name stuck. Abram the Hebrew went on to become the founding father, patriarch, and leader of the "Hebrew" people. So, as a result, the unknown language that Abram spoke came to be known as Hebrew.

When Abram left Haran with his family and possessions, he was joined by his nephew Lot and his family and all of their possessions as well. Their journey took them along the eastern side of the Mediterranean Sea through Damascus and eventually into the Land of Canaan. When they arrived in the Land of Canaan, God appeared to Abram once again and made a covenant with him. God told him that he would be the father of a multitude of nations and that the land of Canaan would be given to him and his descendants. After making this covenant with Abram, God changed his name to Abraham.

> *And I will make my covenant between me and you and will multiply you exceedingly. Then Abram fell on his face; and God said to him, "Behold, my covenant is with you and you shall be the father of a multitude of nations. No longer shall your name be Abram, but your name shall be Abraham; for I have made you the father of a multitude of nations."*
>
> Genesis 17:2-5

In the Bible, a person's name is his identity. The name Abram means "high father" and it identifies Abram as the patriarch and leader of the Hebrew nation. But, as noted in the scripture passage, the name Abraham means "father of a multitude". When God made the covenant with Abram and told him that he would be the father of a multitude of nations, not just the Hebrew nation, his identity was changed. Abram needed a new name to correspond with his new identity. So, God changed his name from Abram to Abraham.

Abraham was a herder and a nomad who moved from place to place. The land of Canaan, which was inhabited by the Canaanites, was experiencing a famine when Abraham first arrived. Because of the famine, he did not settle in Canaan, instead, he continued his journey beyond the land of Canaan and settled in Egypt. After the famine in Canaan was over, Abraham left Egypt and returned to Canaan, the Promised Land, with his wife Sarai and his nephew Lot.

As the decades passed, Sarai was still barren but Abraham believed that God would give him a son as He had promised. You may recall that Abraham was 75 years old when God told him that he was going to be the father of a multitude of nations. It is obvious that Abraham and Sarai needed to have children before God's promise could come to pass.

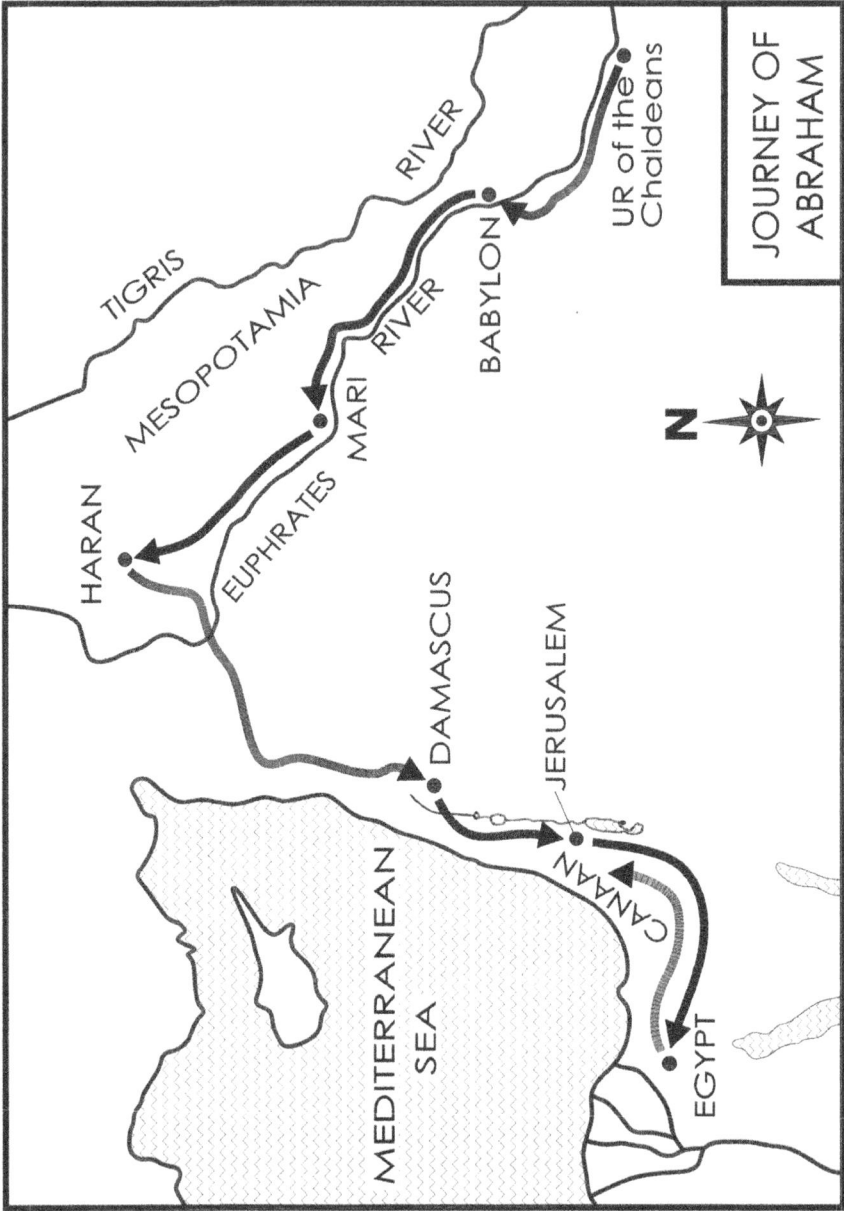

JOURNEY OF ABRAHAM

Finally, when Abraham was 99 years old God appeared to him again. That was almost 25 years after his name was changed to Abraham when God told him that he was going to be the father of a multitude of nations. Now, in this new appearance, God changed Sarai's name to Sarah and He told Abraham that she was going to conceive and give him a son. The following year Isaac was born and it was through Isaac that God fulfilled His promise to Abraham to multiply his descendants as they grew and flourished.

> *And God said to Abraham: As for Sarai your wife, you shall not call her name Sarai, but Sarah shall be her name. I will bless her, and moreover, I will give you a son by her;*
>
> Genesis 17:15-16

As I focused on the Jewish culture, I still needed to understand the difference between the Hebrews, Israelites, and Jews. It seemed like they were all related in some way but I was not sure of their relationship. I decided that I had to understand if they were in fact related. And, if they were related, exactly how that was even possible? Through my research, as I just shared, I learned that Abraham was the leader of the Hebrew people but over time, they came to be known by different names. While Abraham was the founder, patriarch, and leader of the Hebrews, his direct descendants in the generations that followed came to be known as Israelites and Jews.

Although the Hebrews got their name from Abraham's origin "from beyond" the Euphrates River, the Israelites were the direct descendants of Abraham's grandson Jacob, the son of Isaac. The Jews were the direct descendant of Abraham's great-grandson Judah, the son of Jacob. This may sound like it cleared up a lot of my confusion, but I still did not understand why the Israelites, who are direct descendants of Jacob, are called Israelites. I did not know where to look for the answer to this question so I turned my research to the Bible. To be more precise, I went to the book of Genesis in the Old Testament. Once again I discovered a name change in the bible. The Bible tells us that Jacob wrestled through the night with a mysterious being until he finally prevailed. The Bible goes on to tell us that the mysterious being was a messenger from God, an angel, and he told Jacob that his name was going to be changed. The angel told Jacob that his new name would be Israel because he was able to prevail over him through the night. Consequently, with the changing of Jacob's name to Israel, his descendants were called Israelites.

> *He took them and sent them across the stream, and likewise, everything that he had. And Jacob was left alone, and a man wrestled with him until the breaking of the day. …Then he said, "Your name shall no longer be called Jacob, but Israel, for you have striven with God and with men, and have prevailed."*
>
> Genesis 32:23-24; 29

The Jews are descendants of Judah, the son of Israel (Jacob) and they lived in the Kingdom of Judah. Note that, geographically, Judah and Judea are the same place. When the Romans gained control of the Jewish empire in 63 BC, the kingdom of Judah was called Judea at that time. The two well-known cities within the Kingdom of Judah are Bethlehem and the capital city, Jerusalem.

As a geographical reference, the Kingdom of Israel is north of Judah. The two kingdoms were split after the death of King Solomon and, collectively, the Israelites and the Jews make up the Hebrew nation and culture as their cultural names represent a specific period of time in the development of the chosen people of God.

When Abraham and his nephew Lot journeyed together from Egypt back to Canaan after the famine ended, they arrived at the southern tip of the Dead Sea. Abraham gave Lot the choice of settling in the land east of the Dead Sea or the land to the west. Lot settled in the land east of the Jordan River and Abraham settled in the land of Canaan, the area to the west of the Jordan River. In the decades and centuries that passed, Abraham's descendants continued to live in the land of Canaan west of the Jordan River.

There is an old saying, "A little knowledge is a dangerous thing." I know that Moses led the Israelites out of Egypt but learning that Abraham left Egypt and settled in the Land of Canaan, that little bit of knowledge had me asking a question about Moses. If Abraham came out of Egypt and settled in the Land of Canaan and the Israelites, his descendants, were dwelling in the land of Canaan, what Israelites did Moses bring out of bondage in Egypt?

Nothing is as simple as we may want it to be. In a nutshell, this is how the Israelites, the descendants of Abraham, found themselves back in Egypt and in bondage. Abraham's great-grandson, Joseph (son of Israel), was sold into slavery by his brothers. Eventually, he was taken to Egypt where he lived as a slave. Note that Joseph, being the son of Israel, makes him a member of the same family of people who were called Hebrews and are now called Israelites.

Joseph, an Israelite, had a God-given gift of interpreting dreams. While he was still a slave and in prison in Egypt, his gift of interpreting dreams won him release from prison when he interpreted several dreams for the Pharaoh. When the mysterious dreams happened as Joseph had interpreted them, Pharaoh showed his gratitude and pleasure to Joseph by putting him in a position of authority over the Egyptians.   Eventually, Joseph became a very powerful leader in Egypt.

Through his position of power, persuasion, and trickery, Joseph was able to get his father, Israel, to bring his entire family and possessions to Egypt. While Israel and his descendants were dwelling in Egypt, they began to increase in number and the Egyptians were concerned and afraid that the Israelites would gain control of Egypt. After the death of Joseph and the Pharaoh who loved him, the Israelites in Egypt lost favor with the Egyptians and the new Pharaoh. As time passed the Israelites were enslaved and mistreated by the Egyptians. This enslavement of the

Israelites lasted for centuries until Moses led them out of their bondage in Egypt to their freedom and back to the land of Canaan, the Promised Land.

During their journey from Egypt to the Promised Land, God gave Moses the Ten Commandments on Mount Sinai and instructed him to build a sacred chest for the Ten Commandments tablets. The Ten Commandments are the covenantal agreement between God and man. The sacred chest that was built for the Ten Commandment tablets is called an ark and it came to be known as the "Ark of the Covenant".

One of the things that I noticed about the leaders of the Hebrew and Israelite people is that they did not have a formal title. The Israelites were made up of numerous tribes and each tribe called their leader father. As I continued reading the bible I discovered that the Israelites began to notice that the other countries surrounding them had leaders but they did not call their leaders father as the Israelites did. Instead, the leader of each country was called their king. Taking notice of this the Israelites turned to God and insisted that they should have a king like the other countries around them.

The Israelites failed to understand that God was their king. They wanted their visible and earthly leader who governed them to be called their king. God was not happy with this request of the Israelites but he granted them their wish. Saul was chosen by the 12 Israelite tribes and he was anointed as the first king of the Israelites and he reigned for 40 years.

After 40 years as their king, when they were in a battle against the Philistines, Saul deserted his people. With this desertion, he lost favor with the Israelite tribes and with God also. Consequently, David, who was from the Jewish tribe of Judah, was selected and anointed to replace Saul as the new king of Israel.

I know that this is moving pretty fast but this brings us to King David who replaced Saul and settled in Jerusalem, the capital city of Judah. Like Saul, David ruled for 40 years also before he was succeeded by his son Solomon. During the reign of David, the Ark of the Covenant, which contained the tablets of the Ten Commandments, was kept in a tent. Before David died, God instructed him to build a temple for the Ark but God also told David that his descendant had to build the temple. God gave him complete instructions and detailed plans to build the temple for the Ark of the Covenant. Since David was not permitted to build the temple those detailed plans for the Temple were passed on to his son Solomon.

The First Temple of Jerusalem, also known as the "Temple of Solomon," was built in Jerusalem by King Solomon during his reign between 970 BC and 931 BC. The construction of this Temple marked the beginning of the time period in Jewish religious history that is known as the "First Temple Period." A little over three centuries after the reign of Solomon, in about the year 600 BC, Israel was invaded by the Babylonians and a lot of Israelites were taken as prisoners. During that invasion, the Temple was destroyed by the Babylonian king, Nebuchadnezzar. The destruction of the Temple marked the end of the "First Temple Period" and the beginning of the Second Temple Period.

The rebuilding of the Temple did not start immediately after it was destroyed by the Babylonians. When Cyrus the Great, King of Persia, conquered the Babylonians he released the Jews from their Babylonian captivity and allowed them to return to Jerusalem. Shortly after returning to Jerusalem the initial rebuilding of the Temple started and lasted for over 40 years. The Second Temple Period lasted from the Babylonian captivity in about 600 BC until the destruction of the Second Temple by the Romans in AD 70.

As I studied and learned more about the history of the Jewish Temple, I made an amazing discovery. I discovered that God gave King David some detailed instructions on how to layout and build the Temple in Jerusalem. I also learned that the layout of that Temple matches the layout of God's temple in heaven.

There are more than twenty Old Testament passages that describe the Temple of Jerusalem and the same number of passages in the Book of Revelation that matches the description of God's Temple in Heaven. I have made a parallel reference to only three Old and New Testament scripture passages that speak of God's Temple on earth and His Temple in Heaven.

Holy of Holies – Exodus 26:25-33 (earth); ***Revelation 4:1-10*** (heaven)

Altar of sacrifice – Exodus 27:1-2; 39:39 (earth); ***Revelation 6:9*** (heaven)

Altar of incense – Exodus 30:1-6; 39:38 (earth); ***Revelation 8:3-5*** (heaven)

In recent decades I have learned that the basic layout of every Catholic Church is modeled after the layout of God's Temple in Heaven.

SECULAR LEADERS AND ROMAN RULE IN JERUSALEM

Although God told Abraham that the Land of Canaan would be given to him and his descendants, it wasn't exactly handed over to them on a silver platter. They had to fight for every parcel of land they occupied. Here we are today; some 4,000 years after Abraham's battles to conquer the land that was promised to him by God and even today, battles are still being fought for control of the Promised Land.

While the Israelite kings reigned as religious leaders, they were constantly battling with other countries and secular leaders that were trying to gain control of the Land of Canaan. The Jews finally regained control of the Promised Land only to be conquered by the Babylonians who, in turn, were conquered by the Persians. Eventually, the powerful Greeks had their turn at ruling the Promised Land also but the Jews decided to revolt against the Greeks and were able to regain control of the Promised Land once again.

While Cyrus the Great conquered the Babylonians, freed the Jews from their captivity, and permitted them to return to Jerusalem, they were not truly free. The Jews returned to Jerusalem out of the clutches of the Babylonians and were permitted to practice their religion in Jerusalem, but they still had to live under the rule of the Persians for more than 200 years. Persian rule ended when they were conquered by the Greeks under Alexander the Great.

The Greeks were in full control over the Jews, but the Greeks were met with resistance when they tried to force the Jews to participate in the worship of their pagan gods. For more than a century the Jews lived under the religious persecution of the Greeks until the Maccabean revolt of 167 BC. That revolt lasted seven years and the Jews were finally victorious. The Jewish revolt was led by the Jewish priest, Judas Maccabaeus as they refused to worship the pagan gods of the Greeks.

It is important to note that for about five centuries the Jews came under the rule of the Babylonians, Persian, Greeks, and Romans. During those centuries, the Jewish culture was greatly influenced by each one of those foreign cultures but they refused to worship the pagan gods of any of them. As my research brought me to the success of the Jewish rebellion under Judas Maccabaeus, I felt relief and joy for the Jewish people. My joy was short-lived as I realized that, somehow, the Romans managed to move in on the Jews and take control of the Promised Land.

Now, I needed to understand how this transition of power to the Romans evolved. As I looked deeper into the Jewish rule after the Maccabean revolt, the consequences of issues in the Jewish family began to raise their ugly head. Two decades after the Greeks were defeated by Judas Maccabaeus the Jewish dynasty of the Hasmoneans was established. It was a monarchy that was established under the leadership of Simon Maccabaeus, the brother of Judas Maccabaeus. This period of the Jewish monarchy only lasted about 100 years and it came to an end with the death of Shlomit in 66 BC, the last Hasmonean Queen.

The Jewish monarchy did not end abruptly with the death of Queen Shlomit. The end of the Jewish rule of the Promised Land had a gradual transition to the Romans. Well, as they say, "All good things must come to an end." After the death of the Hasmonean Queen, her two sons, Hyrcanus II, and Aristobulus II fought over the inheritance of the throne. Unwilling to resolve their personal differences between themselves, the boys decided to invite an outsider as a mediator. In their selfish ignorance, the brothers decided to reach out to the Roman general Pompey to be their mediator. They asked Pompey, a Roman general and statesman, to choose one of them as the new ruler and king. Now, Pompey saw this as an opportunity for the Roman Republic to infiltrate the Jewish monarchy. Pompey evaluated the strengths and weaknesses of the two brothers and, of course, he selected the weaker of the two brothers to be the new ruler and king.

The Jewish people knew who they wanted as their new ruler and king and it was not the brother that Pompey selected. The majority of the Jews refused to accept Pompey's choice and their refusal resulted in a Jewish revolt against the new king. Under Pompey, the Romans came to the support of the new king as their troops marched on Jerusalem and defeated the revolutionaries. In the aftermath of his victory, the captured revolutionaries were executed and Pompey officially installed the weaker brother, Hyrcanus II, as the new ruler, King, and High Priest.

With Hyrcanus II as the new King, he permitted the Romans to have direct involvement in the internal affairs of the Jewish government. That opened the proverbial doors for the Romans and it eventually enabled them to take full control of the Jewish government, Judea, and the surrounding areas.

In addition to the Promised Land, the vastness of the Roman Republic included the territories surrounding the Mediterranean Sea that came under the rule of four different leaders; Pompey, Marcus Lepidus, Gaius Octavian, and Marc Antony. Now that the Roman Republic had full control of the Promised Land, I discovered an interesting development with those four rulers.

Some 20 years after Pompey and the Romans took full control of Judea and the surrounding areas, in 45 BC, another civil war erupted within the Roman Republic between Pompey and Julius Caesar. Pompey was defeated and fled to Greece leaving the Roman Republic with three rulers.

As I read about the Romans gaining control of the Jewish government, I was reminded of the time in high school when we were doing some poetry readings in my 11th-grade English class. We were studying poetry and the story of Julius Caesar, his victory over Pompey, and the assassination of Caesar. Since this was a poem in a high school English class I thought it was all fiction. In later years, as I watched the movie, Cleopatra, I noticed that the names of the characters in the movie were the same as the names of the characters in the poem we were reading in my high school English class. With the story in my English class and the movie being a perfect match, I just knew that it was all fictional until I embarked on my religious research.

So, here is the true story that I learned about Julius Caesar and how it all ties in with Jesus, the Messiah. After Caesar's victory over Pompey, the Roman senate named him dictator for life but some members of the Roman senate did not agree with that decision. A small group led by Brutus and Cassius conspired against Caesar, and less than a year after he was named the Roman dictator, on the Ides of March (March 15th), 44 BC, Caesar was assassinated. It was Caesar who defeated Pompey in battle and, ironically, his assassination occurred next to the Pompey Theater.

Following the death of Caesar, Mark Antony joined forces with Marcus Lepidus and Caesar's great-nephew, Gaius Octavian. Each one of them was the ruler of a different region of the Roman Republic but before long their greed for power began to affect their relationships. After a short period of time, Lepidus was forced into exile and the Roman Republic was now divided between Antony and Octavian.

As their greed for power continued to flourish, a power struggle between Antony and Octavian began to manifest itself. While Anthony had a long-lasting relationship with the Queen of Egypt, Cleopatra; he tried everything conceivable to avoid a war between himself and Octavian. In an effort to improve their relationship, Antony married Octavian's sister. A seemingly excellent plan by Antony but it backfired when Octavian discovered that Antony was having an adulterous relationship with Cleopatra. That put Antony's declining relationship with Octavian into a nose dive.

Meanwhile, the power surge of the Romans continued and before long, in 36 BC, the Roman Senate appointed their own leader, Herod the Great, as King of Judea. At the same time, Antony continued his long-lasting affair with Cleopatra, and the rapid decline of his relationship with Octavian was accelerated when he divorced Octavian's sister and married Cleopatra.

To add more fuel to the fire, Antony wrote an anti-Roman will stating that he wanted to be buried in Alexandria, Egypt upon his death. This was a major insult to Octavian and it caused his rage and fury to reach a boiling point. He never got over Antony's unfaithfulness to his sister but it was tolerated. When Antony's anti-Roman will came to light that was the straw that broke the camel's back. As a result, another civil war within the Roman Republic erupted as Octavian attacked and defeated Antony. After his defeat, Antony retreated to Egypt with Cleopatra where the two of them, at different times, eventually committed suicide.

With the defeat and death of Antony, Octavian was now the undisputed ruler of the Roman Republic. In his new position of power, the Roman Senate gave Octavian the Roman title of "Augustus," which means "majestic," "The Increaser", or "Venerable". Under Augustus, the Roman Republic transitioned into the Roman Empire. In honor of his great-uncle, Julius Caesar, who had adopted him and raised him, Octavian took his great-uncle's name, Caesar. He came to be known as Caesar Augustus.

As the Emperor of the Roman Empire, Augustus confirmed the earlier appointment of Herod the Great as the King of Judea. This is the same Caesar Augustus and Herod the Great who were in power when Jesus was born. After Caesar Augustus died in AD 14 his successor was also given the title of Caesar. That title became a Roman tradition that was given to each of the 12 successive Roman emperors that followed.

I am absolutely fascinated with the many turns in this story that I thought were fictitious. This true story of the Roman Empire and the secular world has a direct link to the rulers who were in power when Jesus walked on this earth.

Although Caesar Augustus approved Herod the Great as king of Judea, the Jews did not like him. He was ambitious, cruel, and paranoid. In his attempt to win the support of the Jews, Herod married the daughter of a Hasmonean Princess and appointed her brother, Aristobulus, who was only 17 years old, as the High Priest. His plan was somewhat successful. The 17-year-old High Priest became very popular with the Jews but that made Herod jealous. When Aristobulus became too popular with the Jews, Herod had him executed.

Herod had two sons with his Hasmonean wife and both sons became very popular with the Jews as well. Once again the popularity of the two boys made Herod jealous and yes, you guessed it, Herod had both of them executed as well. Augustus was quoted as saying, "It is better to be Herod's dog than one of his children." Finally, in a rage of jealousy over the popularity of his Hasmonean wife with the Jewish people, he turned his rage on her and finished off his Jewish family by executing her also.

Even with Herod having a Jewish wife, the Jews still had limitations with their religious freedom in Jerusalem. From time to time, when I am reading the New Testament, I have noticed that the Jews had to pay a religious tax. Again, I needed to understand why the Jews had to pay the Romans for the right to practice and worship in their own country. The tyrannical rule of Augustus was the same throughout the Roman Empire. The Romans had their own religion, and like the Greeks, they worshiped pagan gods. Anyone living within the boundaries of the Roman Empire was required to follow the Roman State Religion. Everyone worshipped the emperors as gods and deified them posthumously.

True to their form with the Romans, as with the Greeks, the Jews refused to engage in the pagan worship of the Roman emperors and their religious idols. Learning from the Maccabean revolt against the Greeks, the Romans knew that the Jews would never participate in the Roman State Religion. As a compromise, Herod the Great gave the Jews a religious exemption that permitted them to practice their Jewish religion, but in return, they were required to pay a religious exemption tax to the Romans. This is the same tax, also known as the "Temple tax", which Jesus paid.

However, not to give offense to them, go to the sea and cast a hook, and take the first fish that comes up, and when you open its mouth you will find a shekel; take that and give it to them for me and yourself."

Matthew 17:27

During his reign, Herod the Great executed hundreds of Jewish Temple Priests. In the 18th year of his reign, (20-19 BC) Herod did some extensive renovations to the Second Temple. This was an attempt, on his part, to make a form of restitution for the Temple priests he had executed and to win favor with the Jews. Although he was not Jewish, Herod called this renovated Temple the "Temple of Herod". This is the same temple that existed during the time of Jesus and was used by the Jewish people for their religious worship.

The main temple renovations that began centuries before, after it was destroyed by the Babylonians, were completed in 4 BC but additional overall renovations continued after the death of Herod the Great and were not completed until AD 63. In AD 66 the Jewish people rebelled against the Romans again in an attempt to regain control of the Promised Land and after four years of rebellious fighting, in the year AD 70, the Romans were victorious and completely destroyed the Temple. The destruction of the Temple was the fulfillment of the prophecy of Daniel, and the prophecy that Jesus made concerning the destruction of the Temple before His Triumphal entry into Jerusalem.

". . . And the people of the prince who is to come shall destroy the city and the sanctuary"

Daniel 9:26

". . . Jesus said to him, 'Do you see these great buildings? There will not be left here one stone upon another that will not be thrown down"

Mark 13:2

After the death of Herod the Great, the Roman Empire in Palestine was divided into four parts which formed the Herodian Tetrarchy. The term or title of "tetrarch" means one-fourth and it refers to a subordinate ruler who governed one-fourth of the Empire in Palestine. The rule of the empire was divided between the three sons of Herod the Great; Archelaus, Antipas, Philip (from his third wife Malthace), and his sister Salome the First. Salome the First is not to be confused with Salome, the daughter of Herod Antipas.

His son Archelaus was a tetrarch and he Governed Judea, Samaria, and Idumea, which is south of Judea; his other son Herod Antipas became the tetrarch of Galilee and Peraea. It was Herod Antipas who had John the Baptist beheaded at the request of his wife Herodias and his daughter, Salome. This is the same Herod who questioned Jesus when he was sent to him by Pilot.

Philip was the tetrarch of the region north of Galilee and east of the Jordan while Salome the First governed a small region on the Mediterranean coast west of Judea and another small area east of Judea located on the west bank of the Jordan River.

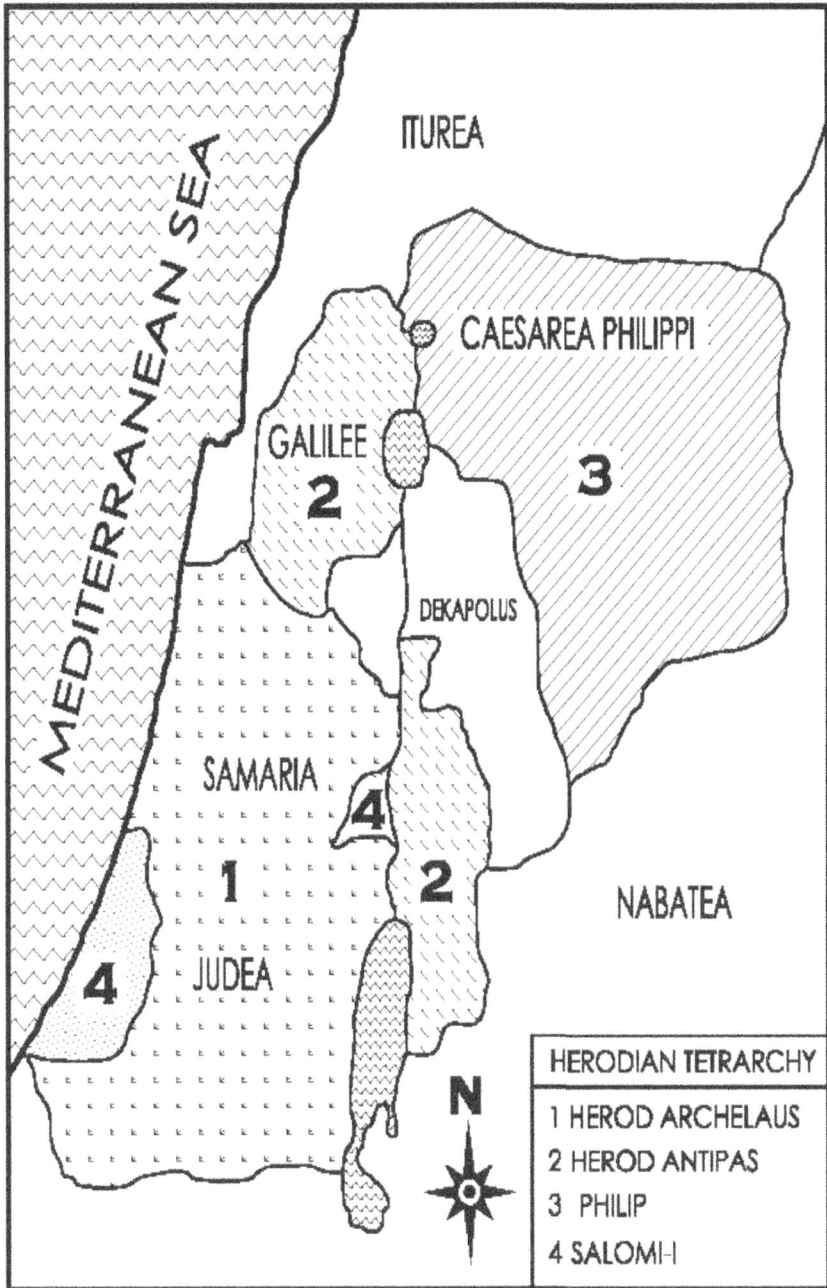

While Herod the Great was alive, Palestine was governed by one ruler and one law. When his three sons and his sister inherited the Roman Empire, they divided Palestine into four regions, and each region was ruled differently. During His life and especially during His public ministry, Jesus traveled through each one of those regions. Jesus and everyone who lived and traveled through the different regions were subjected to the different laws of each region.

CHAPTER 2

JEWISH CELEBRATIONS AND OBSERVANCES

As I learned more about the Jewish religion and its cultural practices, I began to realize that Jewish religious worship and cultural practices were a big influence on modern-day Catholic teachings, beliefs, and practices. Looking back at the Jewish religion during the time of Jesus, I could see that their preparation and celebration of Passover are directly related to Catholic preparations and celebrations of Holy Week, Good Friday, and Easter Sunday.

RELIGIOUS FEASTS

Understanding the religious feasts and observances of the Jewish people can be complicated and difficult for non-Jews. Some of the major religious feasts and observances of the Jewish religion that had a direct impact on the Catholic religion include:

1. Lamb Selection Day

The 10th of Nisan (the first month of the Jewish calendar) is the day that the sacrificial lamb was to be selected for the Passover meal per the Old Testament book of *Exodus 12:3*. The selected lamb is put on public display for five days to be examined by everyone and on Nisan 14 if no blemishes were found, the High Priest would make it official and declared that the lamb did not have any blemishes (no bruises or broken bones). This is the lamb that was slaughtered at about mid-afternoon (between the evenings) on preparation day and consumed in the evening at the Passover meal (*Exodus 12:6*).

2. Feast of Unleavened Bread

A seven-day celebration that begins on Nisan 15 and lasted until Nisan 22. A lamb was sacrificed each evening during the Feast of Unleavened Bread. Each evening the sacrificial lamb of that day was consumed during a Passover meal that followed.

Concerning the Feast of Unleavened Bread, the first day of the feast is a Sabbath day, and the last day of the Feast, the seventh day, is a Sabbath day also. I used to think that a Sabbath day was always a

Saturday but as I studied the Feast of Unleavened Bread in more detail I realized that a Sabbath day can be any day of the week. The first day and the seventh day of the Feast of Unleavened Bread are Sabbath days of rest and they do not always fall on a Saturday.

Seven days you shall keep it as a feast to the Lord;... On the first day you shall hold a holy assembly and on the seventh day a holy assembly; no work shall be done on these days.

Exodus 12:15-16

3. Feast of Passover

Occurs on the only Saturday during the annual seven-day Feast of Unleavened Bread. The Passover Saturday begins after sunset on Friday.

4. Pentecost and the Feast of Weeks

The fiftieth day after the Feast of Passover. For Jews the Feast of Weeks is a celebration of the end of the spring harvest and a commemoration of receiving the Torah from God on Mt. Sinai. They went from impure to pure through self-examination for fifty days in preparation to receive the Torah.

For Christians it is a commemoration of the Holy Spirit descending upon the apostles and other followers of Jesus who were present in the upper room in Jerusalem. Pentecost is the birth of the Catholic Church.

5. Rosh Hashanah

The first day of the seventh month in the Jewish calendar, Tishri, marked the beginning of the Jewish civil year. In a Jubilee year, this date also marked the time when the requirements of a Jubilee year were observed (freeing of slaves, returning of property to the original owners, etc.).

6. Yum Kippur

The Day of Atonement and cleansing for misdeeds. On Tishri 10, the seventh month of the Jewish calendar.

7. Sukkot (Feast of Tabernacles)

Tishri 15, a seven-day celebration that is the commemoration of the exodus from Egypt.

THE PASSOVER LITURGY

For many years I heard about the different Jewish feast days but I had several unanswered questions. My primary focus was on Passover. When and how did this holy feast come into being; and what impact did it have on Catholic teachings, beliefs, and practices today? My research took me all the way back to Moses and the time when he was preparing to bring the Israelites out of their bondage in Egypt. Before he brought the Israelites out of their bondage in Egypt, God gave him specific instructions on how to prepare and celebrate their departure from Egypt. On the night before Moses led the Israelites out of their bondage in Egypt, they ate a meal celebrating their departure and freedom from their bondage in Egypt.

> *And the Lord said to Moses and Aaron in the land of Egypt: This month shall be for you the beginning of months: it shall be the first month of the year for you. Tell all the congregations of Israel that on the tenth day of this month they shall take, every man, a lamb according to their father's houses...your lamb shall be without blemish, a male, a year old... And you shall keep it until the fourteenth day of this month when the whole assembly of the congregation of Israel shall kill their lambs in the evening... They shall eat the flesh that night, roasted, with unleavened bread.*
>
> Exodus 12:1-3, 5-6, 8

So, that celebration meal started with the selection of the sacrificial lamb on the 10th day of Nisan, the first month of the Jewish religious calendar. After five days, on the 14th day of Nisan, in the evening (between the evenings) the lamb was sacrificed, and, that night, which was the 15th day of Nisan the lamb was eaten. That evening, in Egypt, the angel of death killed the firstborn of every household in Egypt except the Israelites who put the blood of the sacrificial lamb on the doorpost of their houses. The angel of death passed over those homes and hence, that celebration meal came to be known as Passover. That meal was a celebration of their freedom from bondage in Egypt and a celebration of the angel of death passing over the Israelite homes with the blood of the sacrificial lamb on their door posts. The next day Moses led the Israelites out of Egypt, across the Red Sea, and into the Sinai desert where they wandered for 40 years in search of the Promised Land.

Although this was the institution of the Passover meal, nothing is said in the Bible about the Passover celebration being observed by the Israelites while they wandered in the desert for 40 years after Moses led them out of Egypt. So, my question is this, "What was happening with the Passover celebration during the 40 years that the Israelites were wandering in the desert?"

Moses told the Israelites, after leaving Egypt, that this celebratory service would be observed in the same manner when they enter the Promised Land.

> *When the Lord brings you into the land...which he swore to your fathers to give to you, a land flowing with milk and honey, you shall keep this service in this month.*
>
> Exodus 13:5

This scriptural passage seems to suggest that celebrating Passover was not going to be observed by the Israelites during their journey to the Promised Land. Possibly, they expected to arrive at the Promised Land in less than a year before the next Passover celebration would be observed a year later. Only two months after the Israelites were led out of Egypt by Moses, they ran out of food and they complained to Moses.

...On the fifteenth day of the second month after they had departed from Egypt.... Then the Lord said to Moses, "Behold, I will rain down bread from heaven for you;"

Exodus 16:1, 16:4

After the Israelites were led out of Egypt by Moses they did not know that their journey to the Promised Land would continue for 40 years. While the Israelites did not celebrate Passover during the 40 years that they wandered in the desert, God worked a number of miracles for them during their journey. God gave them manna from heaven in the mornings and quail in the evening. Now they had bread to eat in the morning and meat to eat in the evening.

Still, the people grumbled against God and Moses as they doubted that God was in their midst. With the numerous miracles they witnessed in Egypt before they departed and the miracles of the parting of the Red Sea, the appearance of manna and quail as their food every day, the people still had doubts about God being among them.

Now that God was giving them food to eat, they started complaining about not having water to drink. At this point, Moses was afraid that the people were going to stone him for bringing them out of Egypt without food or water for their journey to the Promised Land. Unfortunately for Moses, he turned and complained to God about the demands of the people and his fear of them.

...So Moses cried out to the Lord, "What shall I do with this people? They are almost ready to stone me."

Exodus 17:4

To satisfy the people's latest complaint of not having water to drink, God instructed Moses to go before the rock on the Mountain of Horeb and strike it with the rod he used to part the Red Sea. Moses did as the Lord had instructed him and water flowed from the rock for the people to drink. They were ignoring God's miracles as proof that He was among them as they continued challenging God and insisted that He prove to them that He was among them.

> *...They put the Lord to the test saying, "Is the Lord among us or not?"*
>
> Exodus 17:7

In the eyes of God, this was a grave sin. Through the intercession of Moses, God forgave the Israelites for their sin of doubt but there was a serious consequence for their sin. Because the people refused to believe that God was among them, even with all of the miracles, none of the Israelites who came out of Egypt would be allowed to enter the Promised Land. Consequently, they were made to wander in the wilderness until all of the generations of Israelites who came out of Egypt died. It was their descendants only who would enter the Promised Land.

Looking back at the celebration of Passover during the 40 years that the Israelites wandered in the desert, there was another reason that they would not celebrate the Passover. There was a stringent cultural requirement that only circumcised males were allowed to participate in the Passover celebration. After leaving Egypt, the practice of circumcision was abandoned and none of the Israelite descendants were circumcised.

> *Though all the people who came out had been circumcised, all the people that were born on the way in the wilderness after they had come out of Egypt had not been circumcised.*
>
> Joshua 5:5

After 40 years of wandering in the desert and before Moses died, God instructed him to appoint Joshua, the son of Nun, as his assistant and his eventual successor.

As I continued reading the Bible and following the journey of the Israelites to the Promised Land, I could see that their journey was leading them to the east side of the Jordan River. For their journey to the Land of Canaan to continue, they had to cross the Jordan River. When the Israelites reached the east side of the Jordan River, across from Jericho, and before his death God commanded Moses to take a census of the twelve tribes. The census included only males who were twenty years old and older. After adding the census count of each of the twelve Israelite tribes noted in the Book of Numbers, Chapter 26, I counted 601,730. Again, that does not include women, children and the elderly or the tribe of Levite, the priests.

Now I am really confused because I checked a map and the Jordan River is in the path to the Promised Land. I had never read this part of the Bible so I did not know how the Israelites were going to get to the other side of the Jordan River. As I read chapter 3 in the Book of Joshua in the Old Testament, I learned that the Israelites crossed the Jordan River on dry land.

> *...and when those who bore the ark had come to the Jordan, and the feet of the priests bearing the ark were dipped in the brink of the water (the Jordan overflows all its banks throughout the time of harvest), the waters coming down from above stood and rose up in a heap far off,*
>
> *...And while all Israel were passing over on dry ground, the priest who bore the ark of the covenant of the Lord stood on dry ground in the midst of the Jordan until all the nations finished passing over the Jordan.*
>
> Joshua 3:15-17

In my entire life I never heard or read anything about the Israelites crossing the Jordan River on dry ground. I have heard a number of times about the Israelites crossing of the Red Sea but I heard nothing about the crossing of the Jordan. When the soles of the feet of the priest who were carrying the Ark of the Covenant touched the east bank of the Jordan River, the waters of the Jordan River stopped flowing and the Israelites crossed the Jordan on dry ground. This was like the parting of the Red Sea all over again.

After the death of Moses, Joshua became the leader of the Israelites and he led the new generation of Israelites across the Jordan River on dry ground into the Promised Land. They finished crossing the Jordan River at Jericho and entered the Promised Land on the 10th day of the first month of the Jewish calendar (Nisan 10).

After crossing the Jordan River, Joshua had all of the adult men circumcised so that they could celebrate their first Passover in the Promised Land. This marked the resumption of the practice of circumcision and the resumption of the Passover celebration.

> *The people came up out of the Jordan on the tenth day of the first month, and they encamped in Gilgal on the east border of Jericho.*
>
> Joshua 4:19

> *...it was their children, whom He raised up in their stead whom Joshua circumcised, for these were uncircumcised because they had not having been circumcised on the way.*
>
> Joshua 5:5, 7

...While the sons of Israel were encamped in Gilgal they kept the Passover on the fourteenth day of the month at the evening in the plains of Jericho.

Joshua 5:10-11

Recall that this was the exact same date that the Israelites were led out of Egypt by Moses. After the Israelites crossed the Jordan, God told Joshua to remove twelve large stones from the middle of the Jordan River and place them in the camp. These stones would be a commemoration of the Israelites crossing the Jordan and entering the Promised Land.

After the entire nation had completed the crossing of the Jordan, the LORD said to Joshua: Choose twelve men from the people, one from each tribe, and command them, "Take up twelve stones from this spot in the Jordan riverbed where the priests have been standing. Carry them over with you, and place them where you are to stay tonight."

Joshua 4:1-3

When I read the entire Bible for the first time I made some discoveries about the journey of the Israelites in the wilderness. After 39 years of wandering in the wilderness, most of the generation that Moses brought out of Egypt was now dead and their descendants were the new generation that was going to enter the Promised Land. Like their ancestors before them, this new generation of Israelites were chronic complainers also.

I knew about the miracles of the manna every morning and quails every evening for forty years but I did not know about their clothes and shoes never wearing out or the miracle that their feet did not swell as they walked in the wilderness for so many years.

The clothing did not fall from you in tatters, nor did your feet swell these forty years.

Deuteronomy 8:4

I led you for forty years in the wilderness. Your clothes did not fall from you in tatters nor your sandals from your feet;

Deuteronomy 29:4

Having manna every morning and quail every evening for forty years became a very commonplace occurrence for the new generation of Israelites. They stopped seeing these occurrences as miracles and came to expect the manna and quails to be there for them every day. Additionally, I wonder if they ever noticed that their clothing was not wearing out or that their feet did not swell during their journey.

Several Bible passages tell us that the miracles ceased when the Israelites reached the boarder of the Promised Land but in the book of Joshua he tells us more precisely when those miracles ceased for the Israelites. He stated that those commonplace miracles stopped when they ate from the yield of the land in Canaan after eating their first Passover meal. Eating their first Passover meal established the official arrival of the Israelites in the Promised Land.

And on the next day after the Passover, on that very day, they ate of the produce of the land, unleavened cakes and parched grain. And the manna ceased on the next day, when they ate of the produce of the land, and the sons of Israel had manna no more, but ate the fruit of the land of Canaan that year.

Joshua 5:11-12

God worked numerous miracles for the Israelites in the wilderness but there was still one other miracle in the wilderness that caught my attention and I think it may have carried over into our non-religious modern day society. As this new generation continued to grumble against God and Moses for bringing them out of Egypt and into the wilderness, they also started complaining about the food that God was miraculously providing for them.

This was another sinful behavior by the Israelites that was not acceptable to God. Although God still allowed this new generation of complainers to enter the Promised Land, there was a consequence for their sinful behavior. God sent serpents into their camp and many Israelites died after they were bitten by the serpents.

After they acknowledged their sin, the Israelites approached Moses and asked him to pray for them and ask God to forgive them for their sinful behavior. When Moses prayed to God for the Israelites God instructed him to make a serpent and mount it on a pole. God told him that anyone who is bitten and looks up at the bronze serpent on the pole, they would recover from the bite of the serpent.

> *And the Lord said to Moses, "Make a fiery serpent, and set it up as a sign; and everyone who is bitten, when he sees it, shall live. So Moses made a bronze serpent, and set it up as a sign; and if a serpent bit any man, he would look at the bronze serpent and live."*
>
> Numbers 21:8-9

This is the Bible passage that Jesus was referring to when, in the Gospel of John, he compared his crucifixion to the lifting of the serpent in the wilderness when He said:

***And as Moses lifted up the serpent in the wilderness, so must
the Son of Man be lifted up, so that whoever believes in him
may have eternal life.***

John 3:14-15

So today in our modern day society, a serpent that is mounted on a pole is a standard medical symbol. Interestingly, medical science attributes the symbol of a serpent on a pole to the Greek god Asclepius who dates back to 8 BC. The miracle of the bronze serpent that was made by Moses in the wilderness and healed the Israelites dates back to 1400 BC. It may be possible that this medical symbol could have been influenced by the miracle of the bronze serpent in the wilderness that healed the Israelites.

After they crossed the Jordan River and entered Canaan, the journey of the Israelites was to continue until they reach Jerusalem in Judea. The rulers of the towns that were on their path to Jerusalem would not permit the Israelites to pass across their land. Although the Israelites crossed the Jordan River and eventually entered Jerusalem in Judea, they had to fight numerous battles with the inhabitants of the towns and communities in their path.

This is an abbreviated summary of the journey of the Israelites to the Promised Land but it took them approximately 300 years to reach Jerusalem after crossing the Jordan. So, about 300 years after the Israelites crossed the Jordan River and entered the Promised Land, David was anointed as their leader and king. David led them into battle and eventually, he conquered Jerusalem. He would reign over the Israelites as their king for 40 years. When his reign ended he was succeeded by his son Solomon who built the first Jewish Temple in Jerusalem.

The Israelites had to be victorious in numerous battles before they finally settled in Jerusalem. Everything seemed to be back to normal with the Passover celebrations resuming after the Israelites crossed the Jordan River. The celebration continued in Jerusalem for the next 400 years. The Passover celebration was back on track but after four centuries, they found themselves in the crosshairs of the Babylonians.

For decades I heard the biblical name Nebuchadnezzar but I had no idea what or who he was. After launching my research to learn more about the Israelites, that name came up again. I discovered that he was the Babylonian king who conquered Jerusalem in 605 BC and took a large number of the Israelites back to Babylon. To avoid being captured by the Babylonians, the Israelites ran in all directions as they dispersed and fled to different countries, including Egypt. Unfortunately, most of them were captured and taken to Babylon where they lived in exile. Solomon's Temple was destroyed and the gold and silver vessels used in their religious services were taken by the Babylonians. The few Jews who did not leave Jerusalem remained under the rule of the Babylonians while they were in Jerusalem.

The Persians, like the Babylonians, wanted to control Jerusalem also. But, unlike the Babylonians, the Persians were very liberal in matters of religion. When Cyrus came into power as the King of Persia, he advanced on Jerusalem and defeated the Babylonians. Soon afterward he issued a decree that permitted all Jews who were held captive by the Babylonians to return to Jerusalem. They were also allowed to take with them all of the gold and silver vessels that Nebuchadnezzar had taken from their Temple in Jerusalem. Once again, after the Jews returned to Jerusalem, the celebration of Passover was back on track.

> *Whoever is among you of all his people, may his God be with him and let him go up to Jerusalem, which is in Judah, and build the house of the Lord, the God of Israel - he is the God who is in Jerusalem;*
>
> Ezra 1:3-4

CHAPTER 3

JEWISH CALENDAR AND RELIGIOUS NORMS

T he life and religious norms of the Jewish people were focused on the stars and the phases of the moon. Prayers, sacrifices, and times of worship were based on the passage of lunar days, months, years, and decades. In each of these periods of time, various sabbatical periods of rest were established and strictly enforced.

TRACKING TIME

The Jewish method of tracking time is based on the rotation of the moon around the earth. This method of tracking time is referred to as the lunar calendar and their feasts and observances are directly related to the lunar calendar. As we look at a day in the Jewish lunar calendar, during the time of Jesus, it is important to note that the Jewish day begins and ends with the setting of the sun. Unlike our modern-day society, the ancient Jewish people understood this because it was their normal way of life. For us, in our modern-day society, many of the cultural norms of the Jewish religion may seem complicated or difficult to understand because we live by a solar calendar – the rotation of the earth around the sun.

During the time of Jesus, there were three different groups of people living within the city of Jerusalem - the Pharisees, Sadducees, and the Essenes. Each group lived by a different time structure of the day:

1. With the Pharisees, the day was from sunset to sunset (roughly 6:00 pm to 6:00 pm).

2. With the Sadducees, the day was from sunrise to sunrise (roughly 6:00 am to 6:00 am).

3. For the Essenes, the day was from midnight to midnight.

Additionally, The Pharisees and Sadducees followed the lunar calendar while the Essenes followed the solar calendar. It is also important to note that the writers of the Gospels, most of the time but not always, used the time structure of the Pharisees – sunset to sunset. To understand the time references in the Gospels it is important to know which time tracking method the gospel writer is using. Often times the intended audience would determine the time structure that the writers would use.

As I continued on my quest to understand the Jewish religion and culture, I realized that, among other things, I needed to understand why the Jewish people used the time structure of the Pharisees with the day beginning and ending in the evening instead of midnight or at sunrise. For the Jewish people, it was pretty simple because it was a normal part of their daily lives and culture. If we look in the Bible we will see that, when God created the world, the beginning and the end of each day were in the evening. God created the world in six days and rested on the seventh day. At the end of each day of creation, the Old Testament tells us the following:

> ***And there was evening and there was morning, one day.***
>
> Genesis 1:5

That passage was interpreted by the Jewish people as the evening being the beginning of the day. So, in this interpretation, the night or all of the darkness of a 24-hour day was the first half of the day and all of the daylight was the second half of the same day. Before the inhabitants of the earth were created, the earth was covered with darkness. With God, during the creation process, the darkness came before the light.

Unlike a Jewish day, our modern-day is split into AM and PM with half of the day being daylight and half of the day being night. On a Jewish day, all of the darkness is continuous and it was called night and all of the daylight was continuous as well and it was called day.

As I looked into the details of the Jewish day, I discovered that the division of the Jewish day is uniquely different than it seems. They take the total time of daylight and it is divided into twelve equal parts. Unlike our modern-day time structure, with the structure of the Jewish day, the twelve hours or segments of daylight are longer or shorter than 60 minutes depending on the season of the year. The length of daylight and night are seasonal but they are still divided into equal parts. At the summer solstice in June, the days are longer than the days of the winter solstice in December. But during the vernal or spring equinox (late March) the length of daylight and the length of night are equal.

When their time is compared to our modern-day time, the length of daylight and night are not always equal. In their method of tracking time, there are 14 hours of daylight in the summer while in the winter there can be less than 10 hours of daylight. Using the Jewish method of dividing the days equally, the result is that in the summer, the actual number of minutes in one hour of daylight is more than 70 minutes as compared to one hour of daylight being less than 50 minutes in the winter. Again, in the spring, when daylight and night are equal, one hour is actually 60 minutes long. I think that it is noteworthy to point out that Jesus was crucified at the spring equinox, Nisan 15 when the length of the day and the night are equal. This is the month that God established as the first month of the Jewish calendar. I believe that God intended the first month of the religious calendar to begin when the length of daylight and night are equal.

Looking at the structure of the daylight hours in a Jewish day, the entire period of daylight is divided into four 3-hour segments. Those segments are not as simple as they may seem. The time segments were established for the scheduling of religious prayers and sacrifices. I used to think that each of the three-hour segments was given a specific name but in my ongoing research, I made an interesting discovery. As I surfed the internet in search of the Jewish names for the different 3-hour daylight segments, the internet took me to numerous Jewish and non-Jewish websites and all of them were educational to me. While the different websites focused on the prayers and sacrifices that were offered at the different hours of the day, I discovered that the name of the entire period of daylight from sunrise to noon is referred to as morning.

Basically, the first 3-hour segment is a combination of dawn, sunrise, and morning. To get a better understanding of those three segments of the morning, I went to the NASA website to get the scientific aspect and definition of dawn and sunrise. I was using modern-day technology to understand a process that the ancient Jews visually observed and understood without the aid of modern astronomical science.

As it is explained on the NASA website, dawn and sunrise are part of the normal process that occurs as the sun becomes visible over the horizon in stages. The first rays of sunlight will bend as they pass through the atmosphere of the earth. Rays of light that bend through or around something are called refracted light rays. The sunlight that is refracted through the atmosphere of the earth makes the light from the sun visible above the horizon before the upper limb or the first sliver of the sun can actually be seen. This refracted sunlight, by modern-day definition, is dawn. Sunrise follows dawn, but it is not officially sunrise until the first sliver of the upper limb of the sun becomes visible above the horizon.

In ancient times they did not have the precise technology that we have today but they divided the length of daylight into twelve equal segments that they called hours. They simplified the length of dawn and made it $1/12^{th}$ of the total length of daylight. Again, the actual length of that time depends on the season of the year.

Not astronomically but, to an observer, the sun is at its zenith at noon when it is directly overhead. With the ancients, after the sun reached its zenith they saw it as being in a declining phase. This declining phase of the sun was called "evening". Twilight begins when the sun disappears below the horizon and continues declining until the refracted evening sunlight disappears completely.

So, with the ancients, the morning ended at midday and is immediately followed by the beginning of the evening. Also with the ancients, the decline of the sun did not end when the sun disappeared completely. The decline of the sun continued after sunset, twilight, and through the night until the dawn of the following day. So, the hours from noon to twilight of the next day were called the evening, and the time from twilight to dawn was also called evening. In the bible, if an event occurred between noon and sunset, that time period is referred to as being "between the evenings".

All of this may seem to be very tedious, detailed, and complicated but it can be critical in understanding scripture passages that mention a specific time of the day. If we look at the scripture passage in Exodus 12:6, it says *"evening"* in most bible translations. The correct translation is *"between the evenings"* which means the 9th hour or about 3:00 PM. So, scripturally, the sacrificial lamb was slaughtered "between the evenings" and, like the slaughtered lambs, Jesus died "between the evenings". If an activity takes place after sunset and twilight but before dawn, the biblical translation would be referred to as evening or night.

The ancient Israelites did not have the advantage of our modern technology. This caused me to wonder how they were able to track the time, especially during the night. The invention of the sundial goes back to the Greeks in 293 BC but, in the Old Testament, God communicated with Moses way back in 1400 BC. In the Old Testament books of 2 Kings (20:11) and Isaiah (38:8), approximately 700 BC, the sundial or "dial of Ahaz" is mentioned. Before the sundial, the Egyptians used a shadow clock that dates back to about 1500 BC. Basically, the shadow clock was a rod that cast a shadow and the length of the shadow was used to determine the time of day. With all of that, I still don't know how they tracked time after sunset but there was a method that was used to determine the time in the middle of the night. That method of determining the time in the middle of the night is discussed in the next section.

ONE DAY IN THE JEWISH CALENDAR

The Jewish day was divided as follows:

1. **First Hour**: The first three-hour segment of the day *(begins at dawn – about 6:00 am and ends at about 9:00 am - actual time is seasonal).*

2. **Third Hour**: The second three-hour segment of the day *(begins at midmorning – about 9:00 am and ends at about noon - actual time is seasonal).*

3. **Sixth Hour**: The third three-hour segment of the day *(begins at about noon and ends at about 3:00 pm - actual time is seasonal).*

4. **Ninth Hour**: The fourth three-hour segment of the day *(begins at about 3:00 pm and ends after sunset when three stars are visible in the night sky).*

While Jerusalem was under Roman rule, the night was divided into four military watches. Many of the Jews followed this division of the night *(Mark 13:35):*

1. The first watch was *night (about 6:00 pm to about 9:00 pm).*

2. The second watch was *midnight (about 9:00 pm to about midnight).*

3. The third watch was the first *cockcrow (about midnight to about 3:00 am).*

4. The fourth watch was the second *cockcrow (about 3:00 am to about 6:00 am).*

Now, cockcrow is a term that really caught my attention. For a period of time, this was very challenging as I tried to understand the meaning and the origin as it is casually mentioned in the Gospel of St. Mark *(13:35 and 14:30).* My research became very focused as I directed my attention to learning the origin and meaning of the term cockcrow.

Then Jesus said to him, "Amen, I say to you, this very night before the cock crows twice you will deny me three times."

Mark 14:30

I started my research by looking into the crowing behavior and habits of roosters. As I tried to broaden my knowledge of the behavior of roosters, I learned that the Romans relied very heavily on the crowing of roosters. Most of all, I learned that most of the ancient world relied on the crowing of roosters but they only counted the cockcrow that occurred about two hours before sunrise. Unlike most of the world, the Romans counted two cockcrows of the roosters during the night. The first cockcrow normally occurred at or shortly after midnight. The second cockcrow occurred about two hours before sunrise – approximately 3:00 am. The ancient Jewish world as well as other cultures, worldwide, also relied on the crowing of the roosters to tell time at night and in the early morning hours.

The normal behavioral pattern of the rooster crowing is very consistent. During the night the rooster will crow shortly after midnight, every night, then again about two hours before sunrise. So, if sunrise is at about 5:00 am the second crowing of the rooster will occur at about 3:00 am. Wherever roosters are located in the world, they will crow at about midnight and a second time at about two hours before sunrise.

Scientists even conducted experiments with roosters to observe their crowing patterns. They placed the roosters in a dark room and caused a light to gradually come on automatically at the same time every day. After a period of time, the roosters would begin to crow approximately five hours before the light would begin to come on in the dark room (the equivalent of midnight) then they would crow a second time about two hours before the light in the dark room would begin to come on slowly (the equivalent of two hours before sunrise).

While the Romans counted two cock crows during the night, the majority of the ancient world did not specify the number of cock crows. Whenever an ancient culture mentioned or discussed the cock crow, they were referring to the second cockcrow of the night that occurs about two hours before sunrise. Whenever they intended to reference the first cock crow that occurs at about midnight, they would associate that cockcrow with an activity that always occurred at that time such as the changing of the guard.

Each of the four gospels quoted the prophecy of Jesus regarding the three denials of Peter. The gospel of Mark *(14:30)* says that the cock will crow twice but the gospels of Matthew *(26:34)* and Luke *(22:34)* only say that the cock will crow after the three denials while the gospel of John *(18:27)* says that a cock crowed after the third denial.

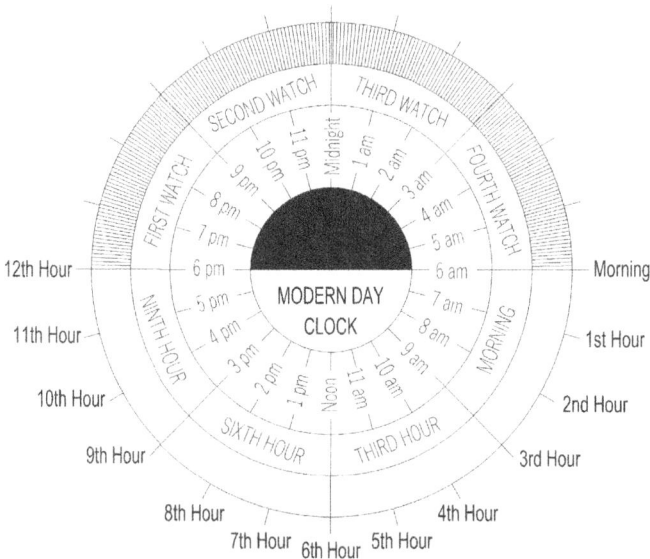

ONE DAY IN THE JEWISH CALENDAR
Jewish day begins at 6:00 P.M.

As I read different internet postings about the cock crowing and the denials of Peter, some of them suggested that the gospels were not in agreement on the cock crowing. One internet post even said that the other three gospels were written after the gospel of Mark and they were correcting the "embarrassing" error of Mark when he referred to the cock crowing twice. One of the primary requirements of understanding gospel writings, or any writing for that matter, is to know the intended audience of the writer and the cultural norms of that audience. Unlike the other gospels, the intended audience of the gospel of Mark was the Romans who always counted two cockcrows. It is totally possible that this is the reason why only the gospel of Mark mentions that the cock will crow twice.

In summary, based on the cultural norm of the Romans and the cultural norm of the Jewish religious community, the four gospels are in total agreement. Each of the four gospels was indicating that the third denial of Peter would happen just before the second cockcrow of the night.

This was a very brief review of the cockcrow term but it was very influential in the Roman military culture and the Jewish religious culture. The morning crowing pattern of the roosters was so consistent that the Romans and the Jewish religious communities used it as a method of telling time at night. The Romans sounded a horn blast that was named after the crowing of roosters. They called their horn blast which signals the changing of the guards the *gallicinium*, which means "cock-crow".

The Jewish religious community used the second cockcrow as a signal to begin the temple preparations for the morning services that would begin at dawn. So, when Jesus referred to the cock crow in reference to Peter's denial, He could have been referring to the crowing of a rooster or the horn blast of the Roman military.

ONE YEAR IN THE JEWISH CALENDAR

While I was looking into the day in a Jewish calendar I discovered that there were a number of calendar-related cultural items that I needed to understand. Taking a closer look at the Jewish calendar, I made a few eye-opening discoveries. Some of them, like solar and lunar, were pretty easy to grasp. To make sure that we are all on the same page; the term solar is a calendar that is based on the earth orbiting around the sun and the term lunar is a calendar based on the moon orbiting around the earth. Although I was familiar with the term lunar year being a reference to the moon, I did not have a clear understanding of what it really meant.

In ancient times the annual Jewish calendar tracked the same time period using two different methods simultaneously. One method of tracking years was the ecclesiastical or religious year of kings and festivals that began with the month of Nisan (March/April). The other method of tracking years was the civil year which has the first month of the year being the month of Tishri (September). Although two methods were used to track years, the year number only changed with the beginning of the civil year in the month of Tishri.

As I continued to look into the details of the lunar year system, I discovered that the first month of the ecclesiastical calendar could not begin before the vernal equinox (spring). This event occurs each year when the day and night are equal in length. Ancient astronomers used the stars to determine the exact time when the vernal equinox occurred. After the astronomers announced the vernal equinox, they waited for the next appearance of the first sliver of the moon. This appearance of the moon marked the beginning of the first lunar month of the ecclesiastical year, Nisan. The first day of the lunar month and the vernal equinox are not always synchronized because the lunar year and the solar year are not the same lengths.

With a solar year and a lunar year, the passage of time is based on two totally different methods of counting months and years. Amazingly, both methods are trying to keep track of the same time period simultaneously even though they are not the same process. The solar year has twelve months and 365 days while the lunar year has twelve months also but the number of days in a lunar year varies between 353, 354, or 355 days. So, the average lunar year has 11 days less than a solar year which creates an alignment problem with religious observances.

Religious observances are based on a combination of the lunar calendar and the seasonal times of the solar year. In reality, the Jewish calendar is a lunisolar calendar; this means that the lunar calendar has to align with the solar calendar.

To help clarify the synchronization issue, let's break it down into a little more detail. This is all very critical because the annual Passover has to be observed as close as possible to the vernal equinox. Beginning with the counting of days, it takes 29½ days for the moon to make one full revolution around the earth which is equal to one lunar month. As mentioned previously, a lunar year can vary between 353, 354, or 355 days, which equals to an average of 354 days for the moon to make twelve complete revolutions around the earth to complete a lunar year.

While the moon is busy revolving around the earth, at the same time, the earth is revolving around the sun. This is the solar method of keeping track of time and it is important to note that it takes about 30½ days for the earth to make one full revolution around the sun to complete a solar month. So, mathematically, a lunar year has an average of 354 days and a solar year has 365¼ days. Consequently, a solar year is about 11 days longer than a lunar year. These differences in the length of years create a misalignment and synchronization issue between the lunar year and the solar year.

Jewish holidays are based on both the lunar calendar and the agricultural seasons, but, as mentioned, those two entities are not always in perfect alignment. Based on the lunar calendar, Jewish holidays are celebrated on the same date each year while the agricultural seasons, which are solar, cause them to fall on a different day each year. Looking at the Jewish calendar diagram on the next page, you can see in note #10 that a 13th month is added to the lunar calendar. This additional month is added to the lunar calendar seven times in every cycle of 19 years to realign the lunar calendar with the solar calendar.

JEWISH CALENDAR
The year Jesus was crucified
Based on LAMB SELECTION DAY - 10th day of Nisan
as noted in the Gospel of John 12:1, 12-13

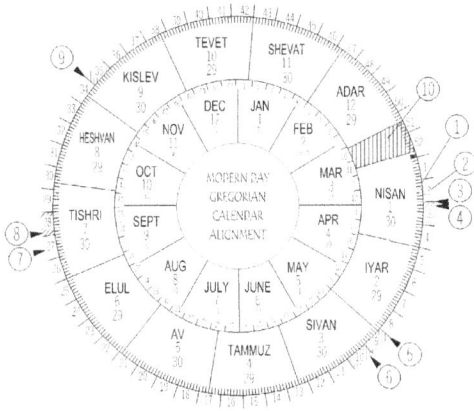

① Lamb Selection Day - Sunday
10th day of the 1st month - Nisan
Week 2

② Day of Preparation - Thursday
4th day after Lamb Selection Day
Week 2

③ Feast of Unleavened Bread - Friday
14th day of the 1st Month - Nisan
Week 2

④ Feast of Passover - Saturday
15th day of the 1st Month - Nisan
Week 3
All 24 Courses of Priest Served
(Course of Abia - 1st Service Week)

⑤ SERVICE WEEK OF COURSE #8
WEEK 9
2nd Service Week for Abia

⑥ PENTECOST
FEAST OF WEEKS
50th Day after Passover
Week 10
All 24 Courses of Priest Served
(Course of Abia 3rd Service Week)

⑦ YUM KIPPUR
10 Day of 7th Month
Week 24

⑧ FEAST OF TABERNACLES
SUKKOT - FEAST OF BOOTHS
15th Day of 7th Month
WEEK 28
All 24 Courses of Priest Served
(Course of Abia 4th Service Week)

⑨ SERVICE WEEK OF COURSE #8
WEEK 35
5th Service Week for Abia

⑩ ADAR II - 13th month added
every 3 years

SABBATICAL PERIODS OF REST

Another aspect of the solar and lunar calendars in Jewish culture is the day of rest. Because God created the world in six days and rested on the seventh day, the seventh day of the week, in the Jewish culture, is observed as a sabbatical day of rest. In the Jewish culture, a sabbatical period of rest goes beyond the seventh day of the week. It extends to the counting of weeks and years with each segment of time having a sabbatical period of rest.

Passover is a memorial meal that is consumed on a sabbatical day of rest. The seventh day of each week is a Sabbatical day of rest. When this Sabbath day occurs during the Feast of Unleavened Bread it is a High Holy Day. This occurs on the day before the first crops of the barley harvest are taken to the temple and offered to God. The next day after the High Holy Day, when the first fruits of the barley harvest are taken to the Temple, is called the Feast of Firstfruits.

After the Feast of Firstfruits, a period of seven weeks is counted for a total of 49 days. This period of 49 days is called the "Feast of Weeks" and one more day is added to the count of days and that 50th day is called the day of Pentecost which is another sabbatical day of rest. On Pentecost day the first fruits of the wheat harvest, not the barley harvest, are taken to the temple and offered to God.

It is also important to note that, in the Jewish culture, sabbatical periods of rest are also applied to the land. A sabbatical year is a cycle of seven years. At the end of the seventh sabbatical year, which adds up to a total of 49 years, one more year is added to the count of years, and that 50th year is called the Jubilee year. The 49th year is a Sabbatical year of rest for the land and the 50th year, the Jubilee year, is a Sabbatical year of rest for the land also.

THE JUBILEE YEAR

In the ancient Jewish culture the jubilee year is a very special time. Throughout the Jubilee cycle of 50 years, the Jews would harvest the land for six years and every seventh year they observed a sabbatical year of rest for the land. Agriculturally, in a sabbatical year, the Jews could not plant or harvest anything for the entire sabbatical year. It was permissible for them to live on the after-growth of the land during a sabbatical year but there was a stipulation regarding the after-growth in a year of rest for the land. It was stipulated that they cannot do any form of cultivation to enhance the after-growth during an agricultural year of rest for the land.

> *For six years you may sow your field, and for six years prune your vineyard, gathering in their produce. But during the seventh year, the land shall have a Sabbath of complete rest, a Sabbath for the LORD, when you may neither sow your field nor prune your vineyard... It shall be a year of rest for the land.*
>
> Leviticus 25:3-5

As I continued researching, studying, and analyzing the meaning of a jubilee year, my learning continued. The significance of the Jubilee year in the Jewish culture goes far beyond the agricultural harvest and resting the land. It is a year of liberation for the land and liberation of enslaved people. All land that was purchased during the Jubilee cycle of years had to be returned to the original owners in the 50th year of the Jubilee cycle. Additionally, all enslaved people were set free and allowed to return to their families in a jubilee year. This was a foreshowing of the freedom that all humans would experience with the death and resurrection of Jesus. This freedom that all humans experienced with the death and resurrection of Jesus is the reason that His death and resurrection occurred in a Jubilee year.

Then I discovered that the jubilee period played an integral part in the sale price of land and slaves. The Jubilee cycle of years determined the value of both the land and slaves. The basic value of the land was determined by the value of the harvest it could yield in one year. When the land was purchased, the established annual value of the harvest was multiplied by the number of years left in the Jubilee cycle to determine the purchase price. This same method of valuation was applied to the procurement of slaves.

> *You shall count seven weeks of years - seven times seven years - such that the seven weeks of years amount to forty-nine years... You shall treat this fiftieth year as sacred. You shall proclaim liberty in the land for all its inhabitants. It shall be a jubilee for you when each of you shall return to your own property, each of you to your own family... You may only eat what the field yields of itself.*
>
> Leviticus 25:8, 10-12

THE BARLEY HARVEST

In the first month of the ecclesiastical year, the feast of Unleavened Bread and Passover is the first religious celebration of the year. During that same week, another sacred celebration is observed; the Feast of Firstfruits. In the same way that the Feast of Unleavened Bread and Passover are connected to the lunar calendar, the Feast of Firstfruits is directly related to the lunar calendar and the agricultural spring harvest of the barley crops.

During the autumn, both barley and wheat, among other herbs and legumes, were planted. At the harvest, nothing could be consumed until the "first fruits" of the first harvest were taken to the temple and offered back to God. Since barley, by nature, was the first crop to mature, it was harvested before any of the other crops. The first harvest or the "first fruits" of the barley harvest was used as the temple offering.

It all sounds pretty simple but it is much more complicated than it sounds. As noted earlier, the ancient astronomers used the stars to determine when the night and the day were the same length - the vernal (spring) equinox. This would determine the first day of the first month of the ecclesiastical year. In conjunction with the stars and the moon, the ripening of the barley crops was also used to establish the first month of the Jewish calendar. After the first barley crop was declared ripe and ready for harvest, the barley harvest would begin. The harvested barley was stored in silos as the people waited for the vernal equinox to be announced. After the vernal equinox was announced the next step was to wait for the first sliver of the moon to appear. As the dark of the moon passed, the first visible sliver of the moon established the first day of the first month of the Jewish calendar.

God stipulated that the first harvest had to be taken to the temple and offered to him before any of the harvests could be consumed by the people. It was also stipulated that the offering of the Firstfruits of the first harvest had to be made on the first day after the Passover Sabbath day that occurs during the Feast of Unleavened Bread. The Feast of Unleavened Bread lasted for seven days and the annual Passover Sabbath would always fall within those seven days of the feast. On the next day after the Passover Sabbath, the Feast of Firstfruits, the first harvest of the barley crop is taken to the temple and offered to God.

The basic timeline between the first harvest of barley and the offering of the first fruits of the harvest is as follows:

1. The barley is declared ripe and ready for harvesting.

2. The harvesting begins and continues while the astronomers watch the stars.

3. The vernal (spring) equinox is announced then they observed the phases of the moon.

4. As the dark of the moon passes, the first sliver of the moon appears and the first day of the first month in the lunar calendar is declared.

5. If the lunar calendar and the solar calendar are too far out of synch, the thirteenth or leap month is added to the lunar calendar at this time of the year. It brings the lunar calendar back into synchronization with the solar calendar and prevents the harvested barley from staying in the silos too long which introduces the risk of spoiling.

With the Feast of Unleavened Bread beginning on the 15th day of the first month, Nisan, the first harvest could not be offered in the Temple until the middle of the month. So, the Feast of Unleavened Bread, Passover, and the Feast of Firstfruits are all connected and take place during the second week of the first month of the Jewish calendar.

The choicest Firstfruits of your soil you shall bring to the house of the LORD, your God.

Exodus 34:26

DAILY OFFERINGS

Before the Babylonian captivity, two lambs were offered in the Temple every day; one in the morning and one between the evenings (in the afternoon). During the Babylonian captivity, the sacrificial lamb offerings at the Temple were disrupted. But, as we move forward into the first century, we find that the practice of sacrificing lambs at the Temple had returned to normal in Jerusalem. The daily offering of two lambs per day was resumed together with the observances of Passover, the Feasts of Unleavened Bread, and the Feast of Firstfruits.

The daily sacrifice of two lambs in the Temple was called the "Tamid Sacrifice". The Hebrew word Tamid means "perpetual, standing, and/or continuing." That means that this offering has to be made every day, for ever. In the third hour (between 9:00 am and noon) the Temple priest slaughtered a lamb and placed it on the fire of the altar as the first sacrifice of the day. The lamb would burn on the fire all day – a continual burnt sacrifice. The offering of the first lamb in the third hour corresponds to the time frame when Jesus was nailed to the cross.

As outlined in the ancient Jewish Mishnah and Talmud, prayers were being offered throughout the entire day while the first Tamid Sacrifice burned on the altar. Together with other offerings that were placed on the burning lamb, prayers were being offered, for redemption, the forgiveness of sins, the coming of the Messiah, and the resurrection of the dead.

In the ninth hour (between the evenings – about 2:30 pm to 5:00 pm), a second lamb was sacrificed and placed on the same fire of the altar. The Tamid Sacrifice of the second lamb occurred during the exact time frame that Jesus died on the cross. Both lambs would remain on the altar and burn all night. The next morning the priest would remove the ashes and the sacrificial process repeated again, beginning at the third hour of the day with the sacrifice of the first lamb.

It was a religious requirement that the sacrificial lambs had to be "perfect". This was determined by a visual examination as the lamb was examined for broken bones or bruises. Even without any broken bones or bruises, in reality, the sacrificial lamb was not a perfect creature. For that reason, a Tamid sacrifice had to be made every day.

Jesus, on the other hand, was our Sacrificial Lamb and He was perfect in every way. Our Lord was the "perfect" Tamid Sacrifice and because of His perfection, His death on the cross ended the requirement of the daily Tamid offering of a sacrificial lamb in the Temple. As a continuation of the daily Tamid Sacrifice, Mass is offered every day in the Catholic tradition.

> *The Mass is the Eucharistic Liturgy of the Church and remains a holy Sacrifice because it is a sharing in the one Sacrifice of Christ, which is re-presented, or made present among us, each time the Eucharist is celebrated.*
>
> Didache Bible, 2001 edition, page 1405

> *Now, this is what you shall offer upon the altar: Two lambs a year old day by day continually. One lamb you shall offer in the morning and the other lamb you shall offer in the evening.*
>
> Exodus 29:38-39

THE SACRIFICIAL LAMBS

The sacrificial lambs that were used in the Temple offerings in Jerusalem had to be born and raised in Bethlehem and they had to be one year old. In the scripture passage below, the offering, by definition, could be a lamb or a sheep. It could even be a bull or goat if it meets the age requirement of one year old or less.

> *And the Lord said to Moses, "When a bull or sheep or goat is born, it shall remain seven days with its mother; and from the eight-day on it shall be acceptable as an offering by fire to the Lord."*
>
> Leviticus 22:26-27

But I kept asking and wondering, why Bethlehem? Was it coincidental that Jesus and the sacrificial lambs were both born in Bethlehem? Going back to the Old Testament, in the book of Genesis, I was reminded that God promised a redeemer immediately after the fall of Adam and Eve. Generations and centuries passed before God revealed to us, through the prophet Micah, in the Old Testament, that the redeemer would be born in Bethlehem.

> *But you, O Bethlehem Ephrathah, who are little to be among the clans of Judah, from you shall come forth for me one who is to be ruler in Israel, whose origin is from of old, from ancient days.*
>
> Micah 5:2

As I searched the internet looking for information on the sacrificial lambs in Bethlehem I made some interesting discoveries about lambs. A lot of websites were trying to use the birthing period of lambs to determine when Jesus was born.

Although this narrative is not about the birth of Jesus, the lambing issue is still applicable. The lambs that are used for the temple offerings are not the traditional lambs that we may be familiar with. Instead, they are the Awassi lambs that are indigenous to the Bethlehem area. While the traditional lambs give birth only once a year and at the same time period each year, the Awassi lambs can give birth at different times of the year. This is important because, as noted in the previous section, two lambs are sacrificed in the temple every day of the year. To satisfy that sacrificial requirement, the supply of lambs had to be continuous and enormous. In other words, lambs had to be born throughout the year to meet the demand for sacrificial lambs.

As humans, we cannot choose our parents or the time and place of our birth. But our redeemer, Jesus, through His Providential Will, chose Mary to be his mother and, in addition to choosing Mary as His mother and Joseph as His guardian, He also chose Bethlehem as the place of His human birth. Jesus was not born in Bethlehem because the sacrificial lambs were born there, but it is just the opposite. The sacrificial lambs were born in Bethlehem because they were a foreshadowing of the birthplace of Jesus, the perfect sacrificial lamb that would be born there. In the New Testament Jesus said that He is the bread from heaven. I do not believe that it was a coincidence that Jesus, the bread from heaven, was born in the town of Bethlehem which means "house of bread".

Jesus is the perfect sacrificial Lamb who came to us directly from heaven. The sacrificial lambs, by human standards, had to be as perfect as possible but, as we all know, they were not perfect. These lambs, although they were not perfect by divine standards, were still very special, very valuable and they had to be protected. In ancient times there were watchtowers in Bethlehem that were used as a military post that overlooked the surrounding area to protect the inhabitants against possible invaders. Over time, the watchtowers were not needed and they were abandoned by the military.

In the construction of a watchtower, the area inside and at the base of the tower was the living quarters for the soldiers. The shepherds used the abandoned military watchtowers as a lookout station to protect their lambs from thieves. The watchtower was one of the places where the shepherds would bring the newborn lambs to protect them from inclement weather. The watchtower also proved to be an excellent venue for lambing as well as the perfect lookout post for the shepherds. As a result, the watchtowers became one of the many places where the sacrificial lambs were born. All of the lambs were under the close observation and protection of the shepherds. Since the sacrificial lambs were very valuable, they had to be protected from being harmed or stolen.

There may have been other outlook towers in the area but one outlook tower in particular was given a name. This special tower was called **_Migdal Edar_** which is Hebrew for **_Tower of the Flock_**. In the Old Testament, Micah prophesied that this will be the birthplace of the Messiah.

> *And you, O tower of the flock, hill of daughter Zion! To you it shall come: the former dominion shall be restored, the reign of daughter Jerusalem.*
>
> Micah 4:8

Providing lambs for the Temple sacrifices was a very big business. In addition to their high social status, the Sadducees had the religious responsibilities of maintaining the Temple in Jerusalem and providing the sacrificial animals. The lambs were owned by the Sadducees and the shepherds were specially trained to take care of the sacrificial lambs. The shepherds may have been Sadducees or even a class of priests. With their knowledge and training, it is also possible that they were familiar with the prophecy of Micah and knew that the Messiah would be born in the "Tower of the Flock."

With the very stringent requirement that the lambs had to be without blemish, a sacrificial lamb was not allowed to have any bruises or broken bones. Those imperfections would prevent a lamb from being sold as a Temple sacrifice. Additionally, the birthing or lambing area of the lambs had to be kept very clean and sanitary. They were located in the lower section of the watchtower and other caves and grottos in the area to protect them from the environmental elements.

Immediately after birth, a lamb was protected from injuring itself, due to its restlessness, by wrapping it in a *__swaddling cloth__*. A swaddling cloth is very similar to the modern-day fabric we call cheesecloth. While it was wrapped in the swaddling cloth the lamb was placed in a *__manger__* for several days until it calmed down and became acclimated to the environment.

Note that there are several translated meanings for the Hebrew word *"manger"*. It can be translated as a *"stall, stable or corral."* The typical manger had a ledge or horizontal shelf projection for hay or other food for the animals. So the lambs were wrapped in a swaddling cloth and placed in a manger or corral for several days. In the same way that the sacrificial lambs were wrapped in swaddling clothes at birth, Jesus was wrapped in swaddling clothes at His birth. At the birth of Jesus, the angels appeared to the shepherds and told them:

> *And this will be a sign for you: you will find an infant wrapped in swaddling clothes and lying in a manger.*
>
> Luke 2:12

Tower of the Flock

Now, when the angels appeared to the shepherds, they were telling them that the prophecy of Micah had been fulfilled. When the angels told the shepherds, *"...this will be a sign for you,"* this was their first clue in locating the newborn Messiah. Telling them that *"...an infant wrapped in swaddling clothes and lying in a manger"* was a very powerful second clue. It would not be difficult to find the only human infant wrapped in swaddling clothes and lying in a manger among lambs that were in mangers and wrapped in swaddling clothes. The shepherds were probably familiar with the prophecy of Micah and they knew that if they went to the Tower of the Flock they would find the Messiah.

THE LEVITICAL PRIESTS

As I researched the sacrificial lambs, I was able to see the relationship and role of the Levitical priest in the temple. All of the Levitical priests in the Israelite community were descendants of Levi and serving as priests was their only duty in life. In the second year after Moses brought the Israelites out of Egypt, God told him to take a census of the entire Israelite community. Based on the results of the census, he was instructed to group them by their clans and ancestral lineage. From this census, every physically fit male twenty years old or older was enrolled for military service. All of the men were enrolled for military service except the descendants of Levi. The descendants of Levi were called Levites and they were not included in the census because they were priests and they did not serve in the military. Their service as priests was a lifelong dedication to serving in the Temple.

> *Now the Levites were not enrolled in their ancestral tribe with the others. For the LORD had told Moses, The tribe of Levi alone you shall not enroll nor include in the census along with the other Israelites. You are to give the Levites charge of the Tabernacle of the covenant with all its equipment and all that belongs to it. It is they who shall carry the tabernacle with all its equipment and who shall be its ministers;*

Numbers 1:47-50

More than 400 years separated the time between Moses and King David. At the end of David's rule as King over the Israelites, in the final days of his life, he anointed his son Solomon to succeed him as King. With the passage of the centuries between Moses and King David, the Levitical priest increased in number. David served as the king of Israel for 40 years and before his death, he conducted a final census of the Levites in his kingdom. The resulting census had a count of 38,000 Levitical Priests with their service in the Temple being assigned as follows:

1. *24,000 Priests and Priest Assistants served inside the Temple*

2. *6,000 Officials and Judges served outside of the Temple*

3. *4,000 Musicians and Singers*

4. *4,000 Gatekeepers*

> **When David had grown old and was near the end of his days, he made his son Solomon king over Israel. He then gathered together all the officials of Israel, along with the priests and the Levites. The Levites thirty years old and above were counted, and their total number was found to be thirty-eight thousand.**
>
> 1Chronicles 23:1-3

Each of the assigned classes of Levitical priests was divided into 24 groups with more than 1,500 Levitical priests in each group. Each group was also called a "course" and they had to serve in the Temple on a rotational basis. The length of service in the temple for each course began on a Sabbath and ended on the following Sabbath. During the seven days of service, only one priest in a course or group was selected to burn incense in the Temple. Although only one priest was selected to burn incense in the temple, every priest in the Levitical group was on duty and was required to be present at the Temple during the entire week of their scheduled service. Over the period of one year, based on the one-week service requirement, each course of Levitical Priests served at least two times.

At any given time, during the week, more than 1,500 priests were serving in the Temple area. On the Sabbath day, when the incoming course replaced the outgoing course, more than 3,000 priests were present during the transiting of duties between the two courses. In addition to their rotational scheduled service, all of the 24 courses of priests (38,000) were required to be present at the Temple during each of the major pilgrimage holidays in the Jewish year. That included the Feast of Unleavened Bread (including Passover and Firstfruits); the feast of Weeks (Pentecost), and the Feast of Sukkot (end of the year and gathering of the harvest). In addition to Levitical priests, the city of Jerusalem was extremely crowded with travelers who gathered in the Temple area during those pilgrimage holidays as well. Being familiar with this religious tradition helped me to understand why Jerusalem was so crowded when Jesus made his triumphal entry.

THE TEMPLE OF JERUSALEM

The Jerusalem Temple was the primary gathering place of worship for the Jews. The First Temple of Jerusalem was built by Solomon after he succeeded his father David as the King of Israel. God had given the actual design plans or "pattern" of the Temple to David but God told him that **"building the temple"** would be passed on to his descendant. As the king of Israel, David was a warrior king and God wanted a man who was a king of peace to build His temple. God would not allow David to build the Temple because, as a warrior king, he waged great wars and shed too much human blood. For that reason, Solomon was chosen by God to build the Temple in Jerusalem.

David said to Solomon: "My son, it was my purpose to build a house myself for the name of the LORD, my God. But this word of the LORD came to me: You have shed much blood, and you have waged great wars. You may not build a house for my name, because you have shed too much blood upon the earth in my sight. However, a son will be born to you. He will be a peaceful man, and I will give him rest from all his enemies on every side."

1Chronicles 22:7-9

Then David gave his son Solomon the design of the portico and of the house itself, with its storerooms, its upper rooms and inner chambers, and the shrine containing the cover of the ark. He provided also the design for all else that he had in mind by way of courts for the house of the LORD, with the surrounding compartments for the treasuries of the house of God and the treasuries for the votive offerings, as well as for the divisions of the priests and Levites, for all the work of the service of the house of the LORD, and for all the liturgical vessels of the house of the LORD.

1Chronicles 28:11-13

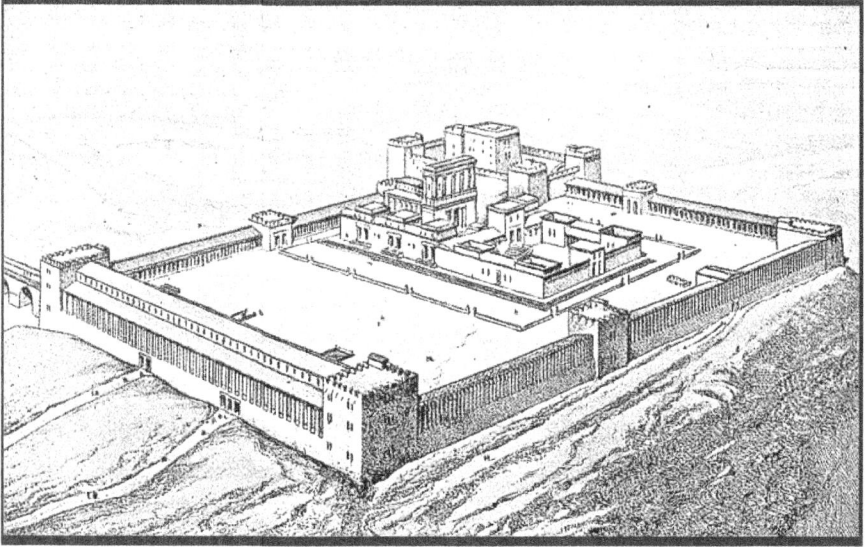

As noted earlier, the First Temple that was built by Solomon was destroyed by the Babylonians. The rebuilding of the Temple was accomplished after the Babylonian exile that ended almost six centuries before the time of Jesus. About 20 years before the birth of Jesus, it was Herod the Great who remodeled and expanded the temple. Although Herod the Great was not a Jew, the temple came to be known as the Temple of Herod because of the magnitude and expansion of the temple renovations.

LAMB SELECTION DAY

As mentioned before, the week before the death and resurrection of Jesus is called Holy Week. After researching and learning about the sacrificial lambs, the Levitical priest, and the Temple of Jerusalem, the events that took place during Holy Week were beginning to become clearer and clearer to me. The first day of the week before Jesus was crucified was Sunday, Nisan 10, and it was a day that was filled with ceremonious activities. Every year on Nisan 10, one lamb was personally selected by the High Priest for the Temple sacrifice and offering. In preparation for this great event, the sacrificial lambs were herded and brought up from Bethlehem outside of the north wall of Jerusalem. They were taken to the Pool of Bethesda where they were washed and groomed in preparation for the High Priest. After the lambs were cleaned and groomed the shepherds took them to the fields beyond the north wall of Jerusalem to graze while they waited for the arrival of the High Priest and his ceremonious selection of the sacrificial lamb.

Selecting the sacrificial lamb was a very ceremonious event with full participation by the Levitical priests and the people who made their pilgrimage to Jerusalem for the religious celebration of Unleavened Bread and Passover. With a lot of fanfare and ceremonious grandeur, the High Priest would leave the temple area to go forward and select the sacrificial lamb. The Temple priest would follow him and line the streets from the Temple to the northern exit of Jerusalem. Remember that this lamb selection process occurred during the Feast of Unleavened Bread when all of the 38,000 Levitical priests were serving in the Temple.

The High Priest processed to the north wall of Jerusalem where he exited through the Damascus Gate with his personal entourage while the Temple Priest lined the streets and remained inside of the Jerusalem wall. Once he was outside of the northern wall of Jerusalem the High Priest and his personal entourage proceeded to the north fields where the sacrificial lambs were grazing and being watched by the shepherds.

After the High Priest made his selection of the "perfect" lamb, he would return through the Damascus Gate next to Antonia's Fortress. As he entered the city, the Temple priests who lined the streets and were waiting for his return would begin to shout:

> *Hosanna to the Highest! Blessed is he who comes in the name of the Lord! Blessed be the kingdom of our father David that is coming! Hosanna in the Highest!*
>
> Mark 11:9-10

Then, when the people heard the shouts of the Temple Priest, they would come out from their homes and the surrounding areas. Running out into the streets with their palm branches they began to shout, ***"Hosanna in the Highest!"*** The procession of the High Priest, his personal entourage and the Temple priests, along with the thousands of people in the city would continue through the streets of Jerusalem as the High Priest continued back to the Temple with the sacrificial lamb. After arriving in the Temple area the sacrificial lamb would be tied to a post and left on public display for five days. The High Priest and the people would examine the lamb for blemishes every day for the next five days.

This is what happened on Lamb Selection Day every year during the Feast of Unleavened Bread and Passover celebration. This entire process of selecting the sacrificial lamb was a foreshadowing of Jesus' triumphal entry into Jerusalem on Lamb Selection Day. And just like the sacrificial lamb that was selected by the high and put on display in the temple area for five days, Jesus would be on display in the temple area for five days after His triumphal entrance.

Unleavened Bread, Passover, and Firstfruits

As I looked at the activities that took place during the week before Jesus was crucified, I wanted to know what was happening throughout that week and the historical meaning behind those activities. Once again I had to go back to the time when Moses brought the Israelites out of Egypt. In their hasty departure from Egypt, they did not have time to add leaven to their bread dough because they could not wait for the dough to rise before baking it. So, in remembrance of their hasty exodus from Egypt, only bread without leaven could be eaten during the seven-day Feast of Unleavened Bread. Based on the instructions that God gave to Moses, the lambs were sacrificed on Nisan 14, "Preparation Day", between the evening (between 2:30 pm and 5:00 pm) for the Paschal meal. The lamb was eaten after sunset on the night of Nisan 14 which, by the Jewish calendar, is Nisan 15.

> *The fourteenth day of the month at evening is the phase of the Lord: And the fifteenth day of the same month is the solemnity of the unleavened bread of the Lord. Seven days shall you eat unleavened bread.*
>
> Leviticus 23:5-7

As mentioned earlier, Holy Week included the Feast of Unleavened Bread, the annual Passover celebrations, and the Feast of Firstfruits. We also know that the first Holy Week in AD 33 came in a Jubilee year because it was announced and proclaimed as such by Jesus.

At the beginning of the civil year in Jerusalem, (September time period for us), Jesus entered the synagogue and read from the book of the Prophet Isaiah. Traditionally, this is when the Jubilee year is officially announced. As Jesus was reading from the book of the prophet Isaiah he was inaugurating the beginning of the Jubilee Year. All debts that were incurred during the previous 50 years were required to be forgiven and everyone who was sold as a slave had to be released and allowed to return to their family. Additionally, in keeping with the norms of a Jubilee Year, all ancestral property that was sold during the previous 50 years was returned to the original family owners. As Jesus read from the book of Isaiah to inaugurate the Jubilee Year, those who were present in the synagogue did not understand that Jesus, our Savior, and King, was officially inaugurating the Jubilee Year.

> *The Spirit of the Lord is upon me because he has anointed me to bring good news to the poor. He has sent me to proclaim release to the captives and recovering of sight to the blind, to set at liberty those who are oppressed, and to proclaim the acceptable year to the Lord.*
>
> Luke 4:18-19

In summary, the Feast of Unleavened Bread is a celebration that always lasted seven days. The first day and the seventh day of the Feast of Unleavened Bread are sabbatical days of rest. During Holy Week in the year that Jesus was crucified, the first day of the Feast of Unleavened Bread was celebrated on Thursday night, which was actually Friday, the 15th of Nisan in the Jewish calendar. This first day of the Feast of Unleavened Bread was a Sabbath Day. In the evening when three stars were visible (about 6:00 pm), the beginning of the next day was announced, which was Friday Nisan 15. Again, on Friday evening when three stars were visible the next day would be announced, Saturday Nisan 16. This is when the weekly Sabbath and Passover are celebrated. This Sabbath was a High Holy day because it was the annual Sabbath that occurred only once a year during the Feast of Unleavened Bread.

For years I struggled with understanding why Jesus ate a Passover meal on Thursday night when Friday night was the beginning of the Sabbath. After reviewing and studying the Feast of Unleavened Bread for an extended period of time it finally made sense to me. To put it simply, Friday Nisan 15 was a Sabbath day and Saturday, the next day, was a Sabbath day also. There were two Sabbath days back to back. I finally understood why the Last Supper was a Passover meal because that Thursday night was the first day of the Feast of Unleavened Bread and a Sabbath day that was celebrated with a Passover meal. This is the Passover meal we call the Last Supper.

The seven-day celebration of the Feast of Unleavened Bread that started on Friday Nisan 15th (Thursday evening) ended on the 21st day of Nisan. The services on Friday during the day included the two daily offerings of the sacrificial lambs. One lamb was sacrificed in the morning and the second lamb was sacrificed in the evening or between the evenings. Additionally, since this day was a Sabbath Day, there was a Holy Convocation service that required God's people to come together and eat a Passover meal.

> *Seven days shall you eat unleavened bread. On the first day, you shall put away leaven out of your houses...on the first day you shall hold a holy assembly, and on the seventh day a holy assembly; no work shall be done on those days... In the first month, on the fourteenth day of the month at evening, you shall eat unleavened bread, and so until the twenty-first day at evening.*
>
> Exodus 12:15-16; 18

In the Jewish calendar, during the Feast of Unleavened Bread, the second sacrificial Lamb was slaughtered on Thursday between the evenings (roughly between 2:30 and 5:00) and eaten at the Passover meal on Thursday night (after twilight). After the sunrise that followed, Friday morning, two more lambs were sacrificed, one in the morning and one in the afternoon, between the evenings, then eaten at a Passover meal on Friday night (after twilight).

While the 14th day of Nisan was the day of preparation for the Feast of Unleavened Bread, the actual preparation for this festive celebration really began on the 10th day of Nisan. This is the date the paschal lamb was selected by the high priest. This day was called Lamb Selection Day or Palm Sunday in our modern-day celebration. On the 5th day after the paschal lamb was selected, Nisan 14, the lamb would be sacrificed in the afternoon.

In the Jewish lunar calendar, like the solar calendar, the same date of each month falls on a different day of the week each year. The year that Jesus was crucified, Lamb Selection Day (Nisan 10) fell on a Sunday. Five days later was the "Day of Preparation", Nisan 14 (Thursday), when two lambs were sacrificed.

Note that in the ancient world, they did not count days in the same way that days are counted in modern times. The ancients did not have a zero value when they counted days. An example of counting five calendar days from Nisan 10 would be done in the following manner:

> *They would begin the counting of days with the 10th day of Nisan as day number one and Nisan 14 would be day number five. Even if it was almost sunset on Nisan 10, it would still be counted as day number one. In a similar manner to Nisan 14, as soon as it is declared a new day after three stars were visible, it would be counted as day number five. This same method of counting days was always used whenever the counting of days was necessary.*

The Passover meal was eaten after sunset, which was Friday by the Jewish calendar and that same Friday was the first day of the Feast of Unleavened Bread which was a Sabbath day. On Friday two more lambs were sacrificed; one in the morning and a second one in the evening. After twilight, another Passover meal was eaten to celebrate the weekly Sabbath.

Because this was the only Saturday Sabbath that was celebrated during the Feast of Unleavened Bread, it was the annual celebration of the only Passover that occurs during the Feast of Unleavened Bread. Per the gospel of John *(19:31)*, it was a High Day. After the annual High Day Passover Sabbath, the next day was the first day of the week and the Feast of Firstfruits as prescribed in the Old Testament.

> *And the Lord said to Moses, "Say to the sons of Israel, when you come into the land which I give you and reap its harvest, you shall bring the sheaf of the first fruits of your harvest to the priest; ...on the day after the Sabbath the priest shall wave it."*
>
> Leviticus 23:9-11

Remember that the first day of the Feast of Unleavened Bread and the day that Jesus died was Nisan 15, a Friday that began at sunset on Thursday evening. The feast continued for seven days and did not end until Nisan 21, the following Wednesday evening or Thursday. This seventh day of the Feast of Unleavened Bread was a Sabbath day also and it was celebrated with another Passover meal.

CHAPTER 4

FINAL JOURNEY OF JESUS TO JERUSALEM

N ow that some of the background information on the Jewish religion and cultural norms has been covered, let us move forward to the time of Jesus and focus on the first Holy Week. The Jewish events that took place in the earlier centuries were a foreshadowing of the events that were going to occur during that first Holy Week. As Jesus embarked on his final journey to Jerusalem, He was bringing His public ministry of three years to a close.

EVENTS OF THE JOURNEY TO JERUSALEM

The Jews did not realize that the annual procession of the High Priest to select the sacrificial lamb for Passover was a foreshadowing and dress rehearsal for the triumphal entry of Jesus into Jerusalem. They also did not realize that their annual Passover rehearsal was about to become the real thing.

With their interpretation of the Old Testament prophecies regarding the coming of the Messiah, they anticipated and hoped that this was the year of the Messiah. While Jesus was about to begin his final journey to Jerusalem, the city was very crowded and in a stir for several reasons.

1. The annual celebration of the Feast of Unleavened Bread and Passover was only a week away and travelers were beginning to arrive in Jerusalem.

2. The Jews traveled long distances to be at the Temple for this annual celebration.

- Some made the pilgrimage every year.
- For others, it was a once-in-a-lifetime pilgrimage.
- The population in Jerusalem would increase from an average of about 15,000 to more than 150,000 people or more.

For seven days you shall celebrate this feast for the LORD, your God, in the place which the LORD will choose.

Deuteronomy 16:15

3. Rumors were circulating that Jesus and Lazarus were coming to Jerusalem to celebrate the Feast of Unleavened Bread.

They looked for Jesus and said to one another as they were in the temple area, "What do you think? That he will not come to the feast?"

John 11:56

4. Many of the Jews believed that Jesus was the Messiah and they wanted to see Him but they also wanted to see Lazarus who was raised from the dead by Jesus.

The large crowd of Jews found out that he was there and came, not only because of Jesus but also to see Lazarus, whom he had raised from the dead.

John 12:9

5. Because of the Roman oppression of the Jews, the entire city was filled with messianic hopes and expectations of a leader who would lead them into battle and bring an end to Roman rule in Israel.

6. Many Jews believed that the Messiah would come in a Jubilee year and they knew that this year, AD 33, was a Jubilee year.

On his final journey to Jerusalem, Jesus left Galilee and headed south. He sent word to Samaria that he was coming but when they realized that he would be continuing to Jerusalem, the Samaritans refused to allow Jesus to pass through their city. The Samaritans and the Jews in Jerusalem were bitter enemies. So, Jesus took a detour and crossed the Jordan before He reached Samaria and went into the region of Judea east of the Jordan. Note that this area on the east side of the Jordan is Peraea on the map but during the time of Jesus, the area just east of the Jordan River was referred to as Judea beyond the Jordan.

After the Roman conquest in AD 132, the eastern boundary of Judea was moved back to the west bank of the Jordan.

Jesus continued through the area east of the Jordan until he arrived in "Bethany beyond the Jordan" *(this is not the same Bethany where Lazarus lived).*

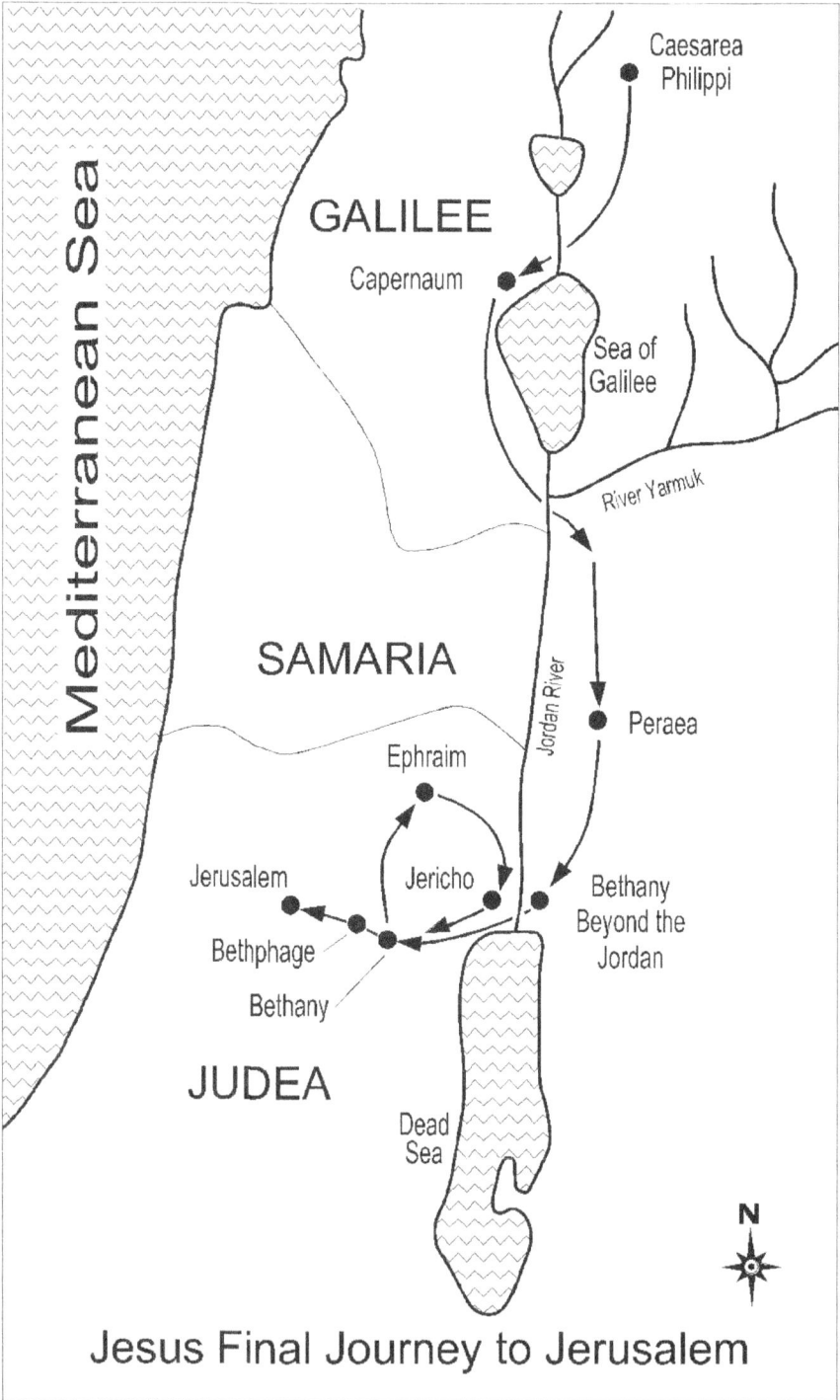

Jesus Final Journey to Jerusalem

This is the area where the Israelites crossed the Jordan with Joshua when they entered the Promised Land. It is the same area in the Jordan River where Jesus was baptized by John the Baptist. His baptism, three years earlier, marked the beginning of his public ministry and now his final journey to Jerusalem was beginning from the same area. The final leg of his public ministry was about to begin from where it all started with His baptism.

> *Now when Jesus had finished these sayings, he went away from Galilee and entered the region of Judea beyond the Jordan.*
>
> Matthew 19:1

The triumphal entry of Jesus into Jerusalem is recorded in each of the four Gospels. Keeping in mind that the events in the bible are not always in chronological order, the sequence of the events preceding Jesus' triumphal entry into Jerusalem is not in the same sequence in each Gospel. We know that Matthew's Gospel, in Chapter 19, tells us that Jesus traveled east of the Jordan where he was teaching and working miracles. As mentioned, this route was taken because the Samaritans would not permit Jesus to travel through Samaria on his way to Jerusalem.

Soon after entering the region of Judea east of the Jordan, Jesus received word that his friend Lazarus was ill but He stayed in the region until Lazarus died. After the death of Lazarus, Jesus crossed the Jordan and traveled to Bethany which is located on the Mount of Olives. He continued to the tomb of Lazarus where He raised him from the dead. Many of the Jews who witnessed this miracle came to believe that Jesus was the Messiah.

After Jesus raised Lazarus from the dead, the Jewish council was looking for a way to put Him and Lazarus to death. Knowing this, Jesus and his disciples left the home of Lazarus in Bethany and traveled northward to Ephraim.

Jesus therefore no longer went about openly among the Jews,
but went from there to the country near the wilderness, to a
town called Ephraim; and there he stayed with the disciples.

John 11:54

Now, with the Feast of Unleavened Bread and the Jewish Passover approaching, Jesus left Ephraim and travel eastward to the west bank of the Jordan River. From there He continued southward along the Jordan until he arrived at Jericho. Jericho is located about 6 miles west of the Jordan River and 13 miles from Bethany. It is a climb of more than 3,000 feet up the eastern slope of the Mount of Olives from Jericho to Bethany. This path of travel was a haven for robbers during the time of Jesus and it is still an unsafe area of travel in our modern-day times.

In the New Testament Jesus tells the parable of the "Good Samaritan" who was the only one who stopped to help a traveler who was robbed and beaten when he was traveling from Jerusalem to Jericho. The story of the Good Samaritan took place on this path and this is the same path that Jesus traveled as he took His final journey from Jericho to Jerusalem.

The original town of Jericho, known as the "City of Palms", is the town that was destroyed by the Israelites after they crossed the Jordan and entered the Promised Land with Joshua *(Joshua 6:20)*. As Jesus arrived at Jericho word had spread that He was coming to Jericho then traveling to Jerusalem. So, large crowds came to meet Him at Jericho where they collected palm branches there and followed Jesus and his disciples as they traveled up the main road from Jericho to Bethany.

And as they went out of Jericho, a great crowd followed him.

Matthew 20:29

As His final journey to Jerusalem continued, Jesus arrived at the home of Lazarus in Bethany on the Mount of Olives. As noted in the scriptures, it was now six days before Passover. This is the Passover meal when Jesus would eat the Last Supper, so the actual day of his arrival at the home of Lazarus would have been Saturday afternoon, the 9th of Nisan. The next day was Sunday the 10th of Nisan, Lamb Selection Day.

> *Six days before the Passover, Jesus came to Bethany, where Lazarus was, whom Jesus had raised from the dead. There they made him a supper; Martha served, and Lazarus was one of those at the table with him.*
>
> John 12:1-2

The path that Jesus took to Jerusalem is shown on the map of His final journey to Jerusalem. As I made the map of the path that Jesus walked on his final journey to Jerusalem, I realized that the crossing of the Jordan River by Jesus at Bethany Beyond the Jordan was a very special place for several reasons:

First: As mentioned, it is the same location where the Israelites crossed the Jordan River when they entered the Promised Land with Joshua.

Second: It is the place where Jesus was baptized by John the Baptist.

Third: The path that Jesus took as He walked to Jerusalem is the same path that the Israelites traveled after they crossed the Jordan River and entered the Promised Land.

As I developed this little map, it gave me chills as I became aware that Jesus was baptized in the same location where the Israelites crossed the Jordan River to enter the Promised Land. Some years ago I was attending a presentation by Tim Staples and in his presentation he said that there are no coincidences in Holy Scriptures. I believe that and I also believe that the events that occurred at this location in the Jordan River were all a part of God's plan.

RIDING A DONKEY

During the time of Jesus, the sacrificial lamb was still being selected on the tenth day of Nisan, the first month of the Jewish ecclesiastical calendar. Jesus was our sacrificial lamb and when He made His triumphal entry into Jerusalem on Nisan 10, the people were waving palm branches and shouting, ***"Hosanna in the highest."*** In our modern-day time, this is the day we call Palm Sunday. This is the day that Jesus was selected as our sacrificial lamb.

As the King of the Jews, Jesus entered Jerusalem on Palm Sunday riding a donkey like his predecessors, King David and King Solomon. He knew that His triumphal entry into Jerusalem as a King who was coming in peace had to be a royal display and it required the traditional prop of a peaceful King; a donkey. Before continuing to Jerusalem on Sunday morning, which was Lamb Selection Day, He sent two of His disciples to the nearby village of Bethphage *(house of unripe figs)* to get a mother donkey and her male colt for Him.

Over the centuries the exact location of Bethphage has been debated. The Greek historian Eusebius of Caesarea places Bethphage on the eastern slope and near the summit of the Mount of Olives. The New Testament says that it is a "Sabbath' day journey" or roughly a distance of about one mile from Jerusalem. A Sabbaths day journey was the maximum distance a Jewish person was allowed to travel on the Sabbath. Also, Bethphage is the village where Jesus cursed the barren fig tree.

Recall that King David was a warring king or a man of war and was not allowed, by God, to build the Jerusalem Temple. While David was king, his son Absalom led a mutiny and took over the throne from him. The new king, Absalom, wanted to get rid of his father and he was looking for an opportunity to kill him. But David, knowing that his son was trying to kill him, left Jerusalem and fled across the Jordan where he lived in exile. After the death of his son Absalom, David returned to Jerusalem out of exile from the east side of the Jordan River where he was hiding from Absalom. David returned to his throne in Jerusalem riding a donkey. Although David was a king of war, now he was returning to Jerusalem as a peaceful king. To symbolize that he was returning in peace, he entered the city riding a donkey.

> *He won over the hearts of all the men of Judah as though they were one man. They sent word to the king, "Return, you and all your men."*
>
> 2Samuel 19:15

When Solomon went forward to be anointed as king and take over the throne of his father, King David, he rode into Jerusalem riding on a donkey because he was coming in peace. Although his brother Adonijah was attempting to usurp his throne, he was not coming to wage war against him. This was a "royal" procession that took him to Gihon which is located at the southern end of Jerusalem.

> *Take with you the royal officials. Mount my son Solomon upon my mule and escort him down to Gihon. There Zadok the priest and Nathan the prophet shall anoint him king over Israel.*
>
> 1 King 1:33-34

When the Temple was built on Mount Moriah by King Solomon, the walls around Jerusalem did not exist. Gradually, as the decades passed, the city of Jerusalem developed, and as the city expanded more walls were constructed. Centuries later, during the time of Jesus, the city of Jerusalem was completely encircled by a wall. Within the walls of Jerusalem, there was an additional wall that enclosed the Temple area.

Jesus made His triumphal entry into Jerusalem by way of the East Gate which was located in the eastern wall of Jerusalem. Once passing through this gate the path led to the east side of the Temple area. Jesus rode the donkey from Bethphage to Jerusalem as the crowd that had joined Him from Jericho laid palm branches on the ground ahead of Him. Like King David and King Solomon before him, Jesus rode a donkey because He was a king who was coming in peace.

As he processed from Bethphage, Jesus was about to enter Jerusalem as the Messiah and King. He was not just any king; he was the king of the Jews. The Jews were tired of being under the proverbial "thumb" of the Romans and they were expecting Jesus to raise an army and wage war against their oppressors, the Romans, and return the rule of Israel to the Jews. One of the interesting norms I discovered through my research is that whenever a king entered a city to wage war, he rode a "war horse" into battle against that city. But if a king was coming in peace, a donkey would be the choice of his ride.

> *And when they drew near to Jerusalem and came to Beth-*
> *phage, to the Mount of Olives, then Jesus sent two disciples*
> *saying to them, "Go into the village opposite you, and im-*
> *mediately you will find a donkey tied, and a colt with her;*
> *untie them and bring them to me."*
>
> Matthew 21:1-2

Recalling the sight of their master riding a beast of burden, the disciples saw the fulfillment of the prophecy of Zechariah that was made more than 500 years earlier:

> *Shout aloud, O daughter Jerusalem! Lo, your king comes to*
> *you; triumphal and victorious is he, humble and riding on*
> *a donkey, on a colt, the foal of a donkey.*
>
> Zechariah 9:9

Although the disciples became aware that this scripture passage was being fulfilled by Jesus, unfortunately they failed to recognize that the beast of burden that Jesus was riding meant that he was coming in peace. The palm branches that were being carried, waved in the air, and placed on the ground for Jesus by those who were following Him were symbolic. They were a symbol of victory, triumph, peace, and eternal life. Palm branches were not placed on the ground or waved in the air for Solomon because his entry into Jerusalem was not a victorious procession but, instead, it was a procession of ascending to the throne of David. While Jesus came in peace riding a donkey, He was fulfilling the peaceful king's prophecy of Zechariah.

> *He shall banish the chariot from Ephraim and the horse from Jerusalem; the warrior's bow will be banished, and he will proclaim peace to the nations. His dominion will be from sea to sea and from the River to the ends of the earth.*
>
> Zechariah 9:9

This is a prophecy of a peaceful king. I needed to understand the peaceful king symbolism in this scripture passage. With the technology I had at my fingertips, I turned once again to the internet for answers. In my research and analogy of this scripture passage, I came away with the symbols of war and peace in this prophecy:

"Shall banish the chariot...and the horse":
He will bring an end to the main vehicles of war which were, at that time, the chariot, and the horse. A peaceful king does not need these vehicles of war.

"Warrior's bow will be banished":
The same is true regarding the weapons of war as they relate to a peaceful king. They are not necessary for a king to rule in peace.

"He will proclaim peace to the nations":

His message will be one of reconciliation.

"His dominion will be from sea to sea":

His kingdom will be extended to include the whole world.

MESSIANIC PROPHECY OF DANIEL

After Jerusalem was captured by Nebuchadnezzar, the captured Jews were taken to Babylon. God revealed to Jeremiah that the Jewish captivity in Babylon would last seventy years. After seventy years of captivity under the Babylonian king Nebuchadnezzar, Jerusalem was then captured and taken from Nebuchadnezzar by Cyrus the Persian king. Cyrus freed the Jews from their Babylonian bondage and permitted them to return to Jerusalem.

> *For thus says the LORD: "When seventy years are completed for Babylon, I will visit you, and I will fulfill to you my promise and bring you back to this place."*
>
> Jeremiah 29:10

The Angel Gabriel appeared to the Prophet Daniel and spoke to him regarding a prophecy of 70 weeks of years. In other words, there are seven days in a week, and in this translation; the formula of one week of years is translated as seven years. Using that same formula, 70 weeks of years would be translated as 7 x 70 years rendering a total of 490 years.

So, the prophecy of Daniel covered 490 years. The angel told Daniel that the Messiah would arrive on earth 483 years after the word went forth to rebuild Jerusalem. But this is a prophecy that covered 490 years not 483 years. Looking at the analysis that follows, the 7 years that are missing are explained. It was a prophecy that the Jewish people knew well and they interpreted the years literally. The scripture verse below is telling us exactly what the Messiah will accomplish when He comes. It is easy to overlook but it is very important to note that those accomplishments of the Messiah would only happen in a Jubilee year.

Seventy weeks of years are decreed concerning your people and your holy city, to finish the transgression, to put an end to sin, and to atone for iniquity, to bring in everlasting righteousness, to seal both vision and prophet and to anoint a most holy place.

Daniel 9:24

Before the 70 weeks of years prophecy can begin, the year that the word went forth to rebuild Jerusalem has to be determined. Once again the internet came to my rescue. In 444 BC, King Artaxerxes issued a decree to Nehemiah *(Nehemiah 2:1-8)* to rebuild the walls around Jerusalem. This decree marked the beginning of the countdown of 70 weeks of years. The angel appeared to Daniel and explained to him how to translate the prophetic timeframe.

Know therefore and understand that from the going forth of the word to restore and rebuild Jerusalem to the coming of an anointed one, a prince, there shall be seven years. Then for 62 weeks, it shall be built again with squares and moat, but in a troubled time.

Daniel 9:25

These are a lot of numbers and it could be boring and monotonous. The Jews relied heavily on the numeric prophecies in the Bible. In their translation of these prophetic numbers, they concluded that the Messiah would arrive at the same time that Jesus arrived here on earth.

This is how the 490 years are broken down. First, they are separated into three units of years:

Unit One: Seven weeks of years is 7 x 7 years totaling 49 years. This first unit represents the time it took to rebuild Jerusalem which began in 444 BC.

Unit Two: 62 weeks of years is 62 x 7 years for a total of 434 years which is added to the years in unit one for a total of 483 years.

According to the angels' explanation to Daniel, the Messiah would appear on earth at the end of this period.

> **And after the 62 weeks, an anointed one shall be cut off** *(this means that he will be killed)* **and shall have nothing** *(this means that he did not die for himself but for others)* **and the people of the prince who is to come shall destroy the city and the sanctuary** *(this is the destruction of the Temple in AD 70).* **And He shall make a strong covenant with many for one week and for half of the week** *(this is 3½ years – the public ministry of Jesus)* **he shall cause the sacrifice and offering to cease.** *(This means that the sacrificing of lambs in the Temple would come to an end.)*
>
> Daniel 9:26-27

Unit Three: The first half of the first week of the 70th week of years is translated as a period of 3½ years. This is the public ministry of Jesus, the Messiah, who would establish His covenant with the people. With His crucifixion, death, and resurrection, Our Lord would end the requirement to sacrifice animals to God. But the Jewish people who did not follow Jesus would continue the practice of sacrificing animals to God. They did not understand that they were redeemed by the Anointed One. But at the end of the

70th week of years or the 490th year after the decree went out to rebuild the walls of Jerusalem, the Temple would be destroyed and the sacrificing of animals in the temple would finally come to an end.

This prophecy could be the reason why the Jews were expecting the Messiah in the year that Our Lord was crucified, but they were looking for a military leader. They did not recognize Jesus as the Messiah because He was too peaceful. Just before Jesus made His triumphal entry into Jerusalem, He explained that the destruction of Jerusalem and the destruction of the Temple were destined to happen because the people did not recognize Him as the Messiah. This prophecy that was made by Jesus was fulfilled when Jerusalem and the Temple were destroyed in AD 70.

As Jesus continued from Bethphage on His journey to His triumphal entry into Jerusalem, He weeps over the city of Jerusalem. He knew that they would not recognize Him as the Messiah or His visitation as prophesied by the prophet Daniel.

> *As he drew near, he saw the city and wept over it, saying, "If this day you only knew what makes for peace—but now it is hidden from your eyes.... They will smash you to the ground and your children within you, and they will not leave one stone upon another within you because you did not recognize the time of your visitation."*
>
> Luke 19:41-42; 44

TRIUMPHAL ENTRY INTO JERUSALEM

Looking back on the Lamb Selection Day section, where the process of selecting the sacrificial lamb by the High Priest is explained, that process was a foreshadowing of the triumphal entry of Jesus into Jerusalem. Jesus orchestrated His triumphal entry into Jerusalem with absolutely precise timing. It was the 10th of Nisan, Lamb Selection Day, and Jesus was aware of the annual lamb selection day pageantry and procession that was led by the High Priest. As Caiaphas, the High Priest, was exiting Jerusalem through the north gate with his entourage to select the sacrificial lamb, the real and true Sacrificial Lamb, Jesus, was making His Triumphal Entry into Jerusalem through the east gate to fulfill the prophecy of Ezekiel. The prophet Ezekiel was given a supernatural vision of the Messiah entering Jerusalem through the east gate.

Then he led me to the gate facing east and there was the glory of the God of Israel coming from the east!

Ezekiel 43:1

The High Priest was outside of the north wall of Jerusalem selecting the sacrificial lamb while the Temple priests lined the streets as they waited for him to return with the Sacrificial Lamb. At the same time, Jesus, the true Sacrificial Lamb, was approaching the east gate located in the east wall of Jerusalem. Remember that the thousands of priests who followed the High Priest to the north gate were still waiting for him to return with the sacrificial lamb. They were waiting to join him in the annual ritual of processing through the city and making their way back to the area outside of the Temple.

The crowd that joined Jesus in Jericho was still with him as well as the many others who joined Him on His journey from Bethphage. As word spread that Jesus was near, a large crowd of people inside the walls of Jerusalem could hear the loud chanting of the crowds who were with Jesus outside of the Jerusalem Wall. The crowd inside the walls of Jerusalem started moving toward the east gate as some of them went out to meet Jesus.

Everything was coming together and the crowd was very much aware of the prophecy of Zechariah that their King would arrive riding a donkey. They also knew from the prophecy of Ezekiel that the Messiah would enter Jerusalem through the East Gate.

Among the apostles who were with Jesus was Simon the Zealot. The Zealots were a political group who sought to overthrow the Roman government and return the rule of Jerusalem to Israel. The war cry of the Zealots was **"O Lord Save Us"** which is a translation of the Hebrew word **"Hosanna".** This war cry is taken from Psalm 118 which is called the "*Great Hallel.*" Just a side note, Psalm 118 is the last Psalm that was sung by the Jews at the end of each Passover meal.

The cries of the crowd with Jesus continued to increase in volume and intensity. The multitude waiting for the return of the High Priest to re-enter the city through the north gate started moving toward the East Gate.

The crowds preceding him and those following kept crying out and saying: "Hosanna to the Son of David; blessed is he who comes in the name of the Lord; Hosanna in the highest."

Matthew 21:9

So they took branches of palm trees and went out to meet him, crying, "Hosanna! Blessed is he who comes in the name of the Lord, even the King of Israel."

John 12:1-2; 12

Eventually, the crowd inside of the Jerusalem walls was caught up in the excitement and joined the multitude of people who were gathering in the temple area. The crowd at the East Gate and the open Court of the Gentiles around the Temple filled the entire area to capacity. Recalling the prophecy of Ezekiel, *"...His voice was like the roar of many waters,"* it is not difficult to imagine the noise level of the crowd sounding like the roar of many waters. It had to be deafening. The shouting and chanting of those who were following Jesus could be heard inside the city walls. Gradually, those who were waiting for the high priest to return through the north gate with the sacrificial lamb started moving toward the sound of the shouting crowd that was following Jesus.

Jesus entered the city through the East Gate and continued into the Temple area and the Court of the Gentiles. The shouts of the crowd continued to increase as some of them questioned the meaning of the commotion. The area near and around the east gate and the courtyard of the Gentiles was filling rapidly. The crowd continued to overflow through the east gate as a large number of them went out to join the Triumphal procession of Jesus.

> *And when he entered Jerusalem the whole city was shaken and asked, "Who is this?" And the crowds replied, "This is Jesus the prophet, from Nazareth in Galilee."*
>
> Matthew 21:10-11

Jesus made his triumphal entry into Jerusalem while the High Priest was about to re-enter the city through the north gate with the selected Sacrificial Lamb. The Pharisees and the Temple Priest were concerned that no one would be at the north gate to meet the High Priest. With that in mind, they told Jesus to tell his disciples to stop their chanting.

> *Some of the Pharisees in the crowd said to him, "Teacher, rebuke your disciples." He said in reply, "I tell you, if they keep silent, the stones will cry out!"*
>
> Luke 19:39-40

What stones was Jesus talking about? I have learned that whenever Jesus spoke, there was always a meaningful message contained in His words. The stones that would cry out could be the stones that the Israelites removed from the Jordan River when they entered the Promised Land with Joshua.

> *After the entire nation had completed the crossing of the Jordan, the LORD said to Joshua: Choose twelve men from the people, one from each tribe, and command them, "Take up twelve stones from this spot in the Jordan riverbed where*

the priests have been standing. Carry them over with you, and place them where you are to stay tonight."

Joshua 4:1-3

While He was still mounted on the donkey, the crowd followed Jesus as He passed through the East Gate and continued to the Temple area where He dismounted the donkey. After dismounting the donkey Jesus did not say anything. He just observed everything that was happening in the Temple area.

The people hailed Jesus as their King in anticipation of an impending battle cry from Him against the Romans. When there were no inspirational speeches or calls to battle by Our Lord, the crowd started to lose interest in their newly acclaimed King. Once again they failed to recognize that Jesus came in peace. The triumphal entry of Jesus was now complete and, after a while, He left the Temple area, exited Jerusalem through the East Gate, and went out to Bethany where He lodged for the evening.

He entered Jerusalem and went into the temple area. He looked around at everything and, since it was already late, went out to Bethany with the Twelve.

Mark 11:11

CHAPTER 5

HOLY WEEK – AD 33

W hile the Triumphal Entry of Jesus was transpiring in the Temple area, the High Priest brought the sacrificial lamb through the north gate and into the temple area. It was tied to a post where it would be on display and examined by the people and the High Priest for the next five days. After five days the High Priest would examine the lamb for the last time before declaring it to be perfect and without blemish.

In the same manner, the true Sacrificial Lamb, Jesus, would be on display in the temple area for five days. He would be returning to the Temple area from Bethany every day for the next five days. He would be on full display as the true sacrificial lamb as He continued to present challenging teachings to the crowds each day in the Temple area.

JESUS ON DISPLAY

Day 1: Sunday - Lamb Selection Day

The city was very crowded with travelers who came to Jerusalem for the annual celebration of the Feast of Unleavened Bread and Passover. The population had increased from the normal 15,000 to more than 150,000 people or more.

> *The next day a great crowd who had come to the feast heard that Jesus was coming to Jerusalem.*
>
> John 12:12

Jesus fulfilled the prophecy of Ezekiel as he made His Triumphal entry into Jerusalem through the east gate.

> *Then he led me to the gate facing east and there was the glory of the God of Israel coming from the east!*
>
> Ezekiel 43:1

Day 2: Monday – Nisan 11

On Monday, the next day after the triumphal entry, Jesus returned to Jerusalem from Bethany. On his way back to Jerusalem, Jesus came upon a fig tree that was full of leaves but it did not have any figs. Normally, figs will begin to form as soon as the leaves begin to appear on a fig tree. Seeing the fig tree with leaves and no fruit Jesus compared it to being deceptive like the hypocrisy of the Pharisees who professed to be very religious but lived a fruitless life.

Jesus cursed the fig tree as a lesson to all of us that a life of hypocrisy will lead to our spiritual demise. After Jesus arrived in Jerusalem He entered the Temple area and proceeded to drive out the merchants and money changers. As the sacrificial lamb, Jesus was totally exposed and examined by everyone as He continued teaching in the Temple area.

At the end of the day, Jesus returned to Bethany again where He lodged for the evening. So, on this day Jesus cursed the barren fig tree and drove the merchants and money changers out of the temple area.

Day 3: Tuesday – Nisan 12

On Tuesday morning, as they were returning to Jerusalem, the apostles saw the fig tree that Jesus had cursed the day before and it was withered to the roots. After arriving in Jerusalem, Jesus went to the Temple area once again and continued teaching.

The chief priests, scribes, and elders questioned Jesus about His authority and the Sadducees questioned Him on the resurrection. Like the demise of the fig tree, He warned the scribes and Pharisees concerning their hypocrisy. Once again, at the end of the day, Jesus returned to Bethany to lodge for the evening.

Day 4: Wednesday – Nisan 13

The next day Jesus returns to Jerusalem in the Temple area for the fourth consecutive day where he continued teaching. He told his apostles that in two days he would be delivered up and crucified. Meanwhile, Judas Iscariot went to meet with the chief priest where he negotiated the betrayal of Jesus for thirty pieces of silver.

After Jesus finished teaching in the Temple area, He returned to Bethany for the last time. On this day the betrayal of Jesus by Judas Iscariot was finalized with the chief priest.

Day 5: Thursday – Nisan 14

It was now the fifth day after Lamb Selection Day. The sacrificial lamb that was brought to the Temple area by the High Priest was still on display and being examined. This is the day that the High Priest will examine the sacrificial lamb for the last time and it would be officially declared as being perfect for the Passover sacrifice. Similarly, this is the fifth day that Jesus, our Sacrificial Lamb, would be on display in the Temple area as well.

Since this was the day of preparation before the Feast of Unleavened Bread, Jesus sent Peter and John to make preparations for the Paschal Meal in the Upper Room. Jesus returned to the Temple area for the last time.

Recall that after Lazarus was raised from the dead, Caiaphas prophesied that Jesus was the perfect sacrifice for the people. So, the sacrificial lamb that was selected by Caiaphas, as well as the True Sacrificial Lamb, Jesus, were both declared by the High Priest as perfect sacrifices.

> ... *"You know nothing, nor do you consider that it is better for you that one man should die instead of the people, so that the whole nation may not perish"...he prophesied that Jesus was going to die for the nation.*
>
> John 11:49-51

Friday – Nisan 15

Thursday, Nisan 14, was the day of preparation when the Sacrificial Lamb was killed between the evenings (between 2:30 pm and 5:00 pm by the Jewish calendar). After 6:00 pm, by our modern-day calendar, it was still Thursday but it was Friday Nisan 15 by the Jewish calendar. This is the time that the Passover celebration would begin and the meal was eaten.

Friday, Nisan 15 was the first day of the Feast of Unleavened Bread and it was a Sabbath Day with a Holy Convocation. This is the evening (Thursday by our modern-day calendar) that Jesus ate the Passover meal with His disciples. So, the 14th day of Nisan is the day of preparation and the 15th day is the first day of the Feast of Unleavened Bread.

> *The fourteenth day of the month, at evening, is the phase of the Lord: And the fifteenth day of the same month is the solemnity of the unleavened bread of the Lord.*
>
> Leviticus 23:5-6

The Last Supper

Once again, I recalled what I learned about the Passover from my research a few decades ago. Back then I wanted to know what took place at the Last Supper. Here is a brief review of what I learned. The Passover meal is divided into four parts with the drinking of a cup of wine during each part of the meal and each cup has a meaning. Here is a brief summary of the four cups of wine that are consumed during the Passover meal.

The First Cup:
The Cup of Thanksgiving

As the Passover meal begins the master of the house rises and gives thanks to God for the wine and the great day. He sits down and drinks the first cup of wine in a reclining posture, leaning on his left elbow. This reclining posture is symbolic of a king or free man at his ease and not as a slave. The others drink at the same time. After drinking the first cup of wine the master rises and washes his hands while the others remain seated.

The master takes a small portion of the bitter herbs, dips them in the salt water, and eats them while reclining on his left elbow. Some unleavened cakes are wrapped and stacked on the table. He removes one unleavened cake from the middle of the stack and breaks it into two pieces. He wraps one-half of the unleavened cake and places it under a pillow or cushion. This portion, called the Afikoman, will be distributed and eaten later during the supper. The other half portion is placed in a dish with the other cakes of unleavened bread that have been unwrapped.

All rise and, together, take hold of the dish with the cakes of unleavened bread and solemnly lift it while chanting slowly in Aramaic, "This is the bread of affliction which our fathers ate in Egypt. This year here, next year in Jerusalem; this year slaves, next year free".

God is praised and blessed for His wondrous mercies to their nation and the first part of the **Little Hallel** *is recited (Psalms 113 and 114).*

The Second Cup:
The Cup of Deliverance or the Haggadah

The first part of the ceremony is brought to a close with the drinking of the second cup of wine. It is held triumphantly aloft and called the cup of Haggadah or the story of deliverance. This completes the introductory ceremonies to the main meal.

The meal proper begins with all washing their hands. The master recites a blessing over the cakes of unleavened bread, dips small fragments of them in the salt water, and eats them in a reclining position. He distributes pieces of the unleavened bread to the others.

He takes some bitter herbs, dips them in the Charoseth (pounded fruits mixed with vinegar), and gives them to the others to be eaten. He puts some horseradish between two pieces of unleavened bread and passes it around the table to be eaten by all.

The supper proper is served. It consists of many courses of dishes such as soup, fish, etc., that have been prepared in curious ways unknown to Gentiles.

At the end of the meal the Afikoman, the other half of the cake of unleavened bread that was placed under a pillow or cushion during the introductory ceremony, is brought out. It is divided between all present and eaten.

While they were eating, Jesus took bread, said the blessing, broke it, and giving it to his disciples said, "Take and eat; this is my body".
Matthew 26:26

(It is believed that during this part of the meal, the distribution of the Afikoman, is when Our Lord instituted the Holy Eucharist by changing the bread into his body.)

The Third Cup:
The Cup of Blessing

After the Afikoman is eaten a third cup is filled with wine. Grace after the meal is said and the third cup of wine is consumed in the same reclining position.

Then he took a cup, gave thanks, and gave it to them, saying, "Drink from it, all of you, for this is my blood of the covenant, which will be shed on behalf of many for the forgiveness of sins.
Matthew 26:27-28

(It is believed that during this part of the meal, pouring of the third cup of wine, Our Lord changed the wine into his blood.)

The Fourth Cup:
The Cup of Consummation

*A fourth cup is filled with wine and the **Great Hallel** (Psalms 115 to 118) is sung with a prayer of praise. The fourth cup is drunk in a reclining position. A prayer is said asking God to accept what they have done and the meal is ended.*

Although the Paschal Meal normally ended with the drinking of the fourth cup of wine, Jesus did not drink the fourth cup of wine at the Last Supper. Before leaving the upper room for the Garden of Gethsemane, He told everyone in the upper room:

Amen, I say to you, I shall not drink again the fruit of the vine until the day when I drink it new in the kingdom of God.

Mark 14:25

THE PASSION AND CRUCIFIXION

After the Passover meal, Jesus led his apostles from the upper room to the Garden of Gethsemane. The length of the Passover meal can be as short as about 30 minutes or it can last all night. The gospels tell us that after Jesus arrived in the Garden of Gethsemane He went about a stone's throw and prayed for one hour. He returned to his apostles twice only to find them asleep each time. He returned to pray saying the same thing a second and third time.

> *Then he returned once more and found them asleep, for they could not keep their eyes open. He left them and withdrew again and prayed a third time, saying the same thing again.*
> Matthew 26:43-44

In my analysis above, I am attempting to establish the approximate time that Jesus was arrested. If Jesus prayed for about an hour saying the same prayer each time, the total time that he prayed in the Garden of Gethsemane would have been about three hours before the crowd arrived to arrest Him. Looking back at the crowing pattern of roosters, the first cockcrow is normally at about midnight. This means that Jesus was arrested in the Garden of Gethsemane and was on trial before midnight.

The first cockcrow would place Peter's first denial at about midnight.

With the second cockcrow occurring about two hours before sunrise, this time-frame would place Peter's third denial of Our Lord just before sunrise. As noted in the Gospel of Luke (*22:63*), Jesus was mocked, beaten, and reviled by the men who were holding him until it was morning. The Gospel of John (*18:28; 19:1*) tells us that it was morning when Jesus was brought before Pilate. From the section on one day in the Jewish calendar, recall that the fourth watch ended at morning which is about 6:00 a.m.

Jesus was arrested in the Garden of Gethsemane, scourged, mockingly crowned with thorns, and dressed in His own garments before being led to Calvary.

For many decades I have heard it said that Jesus was Priest, Prophet, and King. I vaguely understood what it meant but I did not fully understand the meaning of that statement. Now, with my newly acquired knowledge of the crucifixion, I see it in a way that gives me a much different perspective on the Crucifixion. In the past, I did not realize that in the crucifixion, while Jesus carried the cross to Calvary, He was the Sacrificial Lamb of God and the *"High Priest"* at the same time. With my newfound knowledge, I was able to recognize Jesus as the High Priest by the garment that he wore while carrying the cross.

Before they placed the cross over His shoulders they dressed Jesus in His own garment. The garment that He wore was a very special garment that is called a chiton (pronounced *key-tone'*). It was a garment that was woven in one piece and without any seams. This was the same type of garment that was worn by a High Priest when he was conducting official religious services in the Temple - including the sacrificing of the lambs.

In the same manner that the chiton is worn by the High Priest when he takes the sacrificial lamb to the altar of sacrifice, our High Priest, Jesus, was wearing the seamless religious garment of the High Priest while carrying the cross. This specific action made Jesus the High Priest who was taking Himself, the Perfect Sacrificial Lamb, to the altar of sacrifice, Calvary.

The Paschal Lamb that was selected by the High Priest and the true Sacrificial Lamb, Jesus, were both being sacrificed for the sins of the people. After arriving at Calvary, with the cross being carried by Simon of Cyrene, Jesus was crucified as our *"Sacrificial Lamb."* Jesus arrived at Calvary as the High priest, and when the soldiers removed the seamless garment that He was wearing, Our Lord was now the perfect *"Sacrificial Lamb."*

Again, recall that two lambs were sacrificed in the temple every day. One was sacrificed in the morning and a second one was sacrificed in the evening (between the evenings). While the first lamb was being sacrificed at the morning services in the Temple during the third hour, Our Lord was being nailed to the cross at Calvary. While the evening sacrifice of the second lamb of the day occurred during the ninth hour, Our Lord hung on the cross and was about to breathe His last.

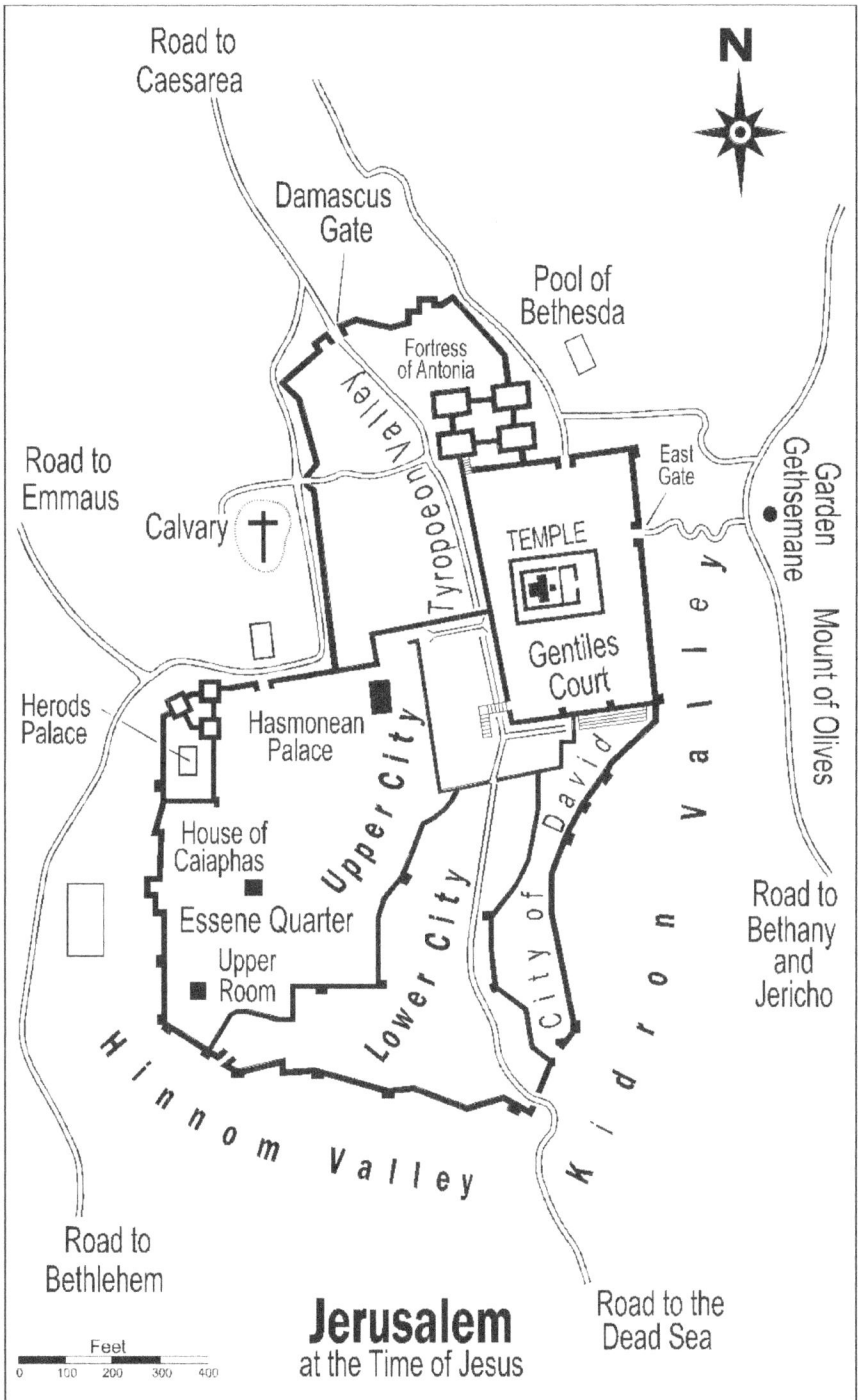

Jerusalem
at the Time of Jesus

Road to
Caesarea

Damascus
Gate

Pool of
Bethesda

Fortress
of Antonia

N

Road to
Emmaus

Calvary

TEMPLE

East
Gate

Garden
Gethsemane

Tyropoeon Valley

Gentiles
Court

Mount of Olives

Herods
Palace

Hasmonean
Palace

Upper City

City of David

Kidron Valley

Road to
Bethany
and
Jericho

House of
Caiaphas

Essene Quarter

Upper
Room

Lower City

Hinnom Valley

Road to
Bethlehem

Feet
0   100   200   300   400

Road to the
Dead Sea

JERUSALEM AT THE TIME OF JESUS

It was the ninth hour when Our Lord cried out, *"My God, my God, why have you forsaken me?"* I was always puzzled by those words spoken by Jesus from the cross. This is a puzzle that I needed to solve. As I proceeded to search for a solution to that word puzzle, I learned that, when praying the Psalms during the time of Jesus, it was customary to say the first line of a Psalm aloud and then continue praying the entire psalm silently.

The lament of Jesus was the *first words of Psalm 22.* It is called the Psalm of the *"Suffering Servant,"* a prayer of an innocent person as well as a *"prophecy of the Crucifixion"* of Our Lord. The cry of Our Lord was a proclamation that He was fulfilling the prophecy of deliverance, victory, and triumph through his suffering. The first line of the Psalm is a cry of desolation that Our Lord prayed:

> *My God, my God, why have you abandoned me? Why so far from my call for help, from my cries of anguish?*
>
> Psalm 22:2

The psalm continues with the lament of the suffering servant as it describes the crucifixion scene:

> *Dogs surround me; a pack of evildoers closes in on me. They have pierced my hands and my feet I can count all my bones. "They divide my garments among them; for my clothing, they cast lots."*
>
> Psalm 22:17-19

As the crucifixion scene is prophesied, the psalm ends with the final prophecy of the Messianic deliverance:

The generation to come will be told of the Lord, that they
may proclaim to a people yet unborn the deliverance you
have brought.

Psalm 22:32

As noted in the "Last Supper" section, Jesus did not drink the required fourth cup of wine. It was very obvious to everyone in the upper room that the Passover meal was not officially finished. A modern-day example of how noticeable it was that the fourth cup of wine was not being consumed by Jesus would be like you going to court and your attorney failed to be present in the courtroom. Would you notice? Would everyone in the courtroom notice? That's how obvious it was to everyone in the upper room that the fourth cup of wine was not consumed but they did not understand why. Even when Jesus told them the reason why he did not drink the fourth cup, they still did not understand His explanation.

Although Jesus did not drink the fourth cup of wine to finish the Paschal meal, He led his apostles from the upper room to the Garden of Gethsemane. From there Jesus was arrested, scourged, crowned with thorns, and carried the cross to Calvary where he was crucified.

On Friday evening *(between 2:30 p.m. and 5:00 p.m.)*, while Our Lord hung on the cross, the second lamb was being slaughtered in the Temple at the ninth hour. Our Lord said from the cross, *"I Thirst."* A soldier placed a sponge on a hyssop branch, soaked it in wine, and raised it up to Him to suck the wine from the sponge. After sucking the sour wine from the sponge, Our Lord said, *"It is finished"* then gave up his spirit.

Note that it was a hyssop branch that was used in Egypt by the Israelites to spread the blood of the sacrificial lamb on the door post of their homes. This was done before they ate their first Passover meal in the evening before Moses led them out of Egypt.

I believe that the meaning of those words that were uttered by Jesus from the cross, "It is finished", is not fully understood by many. On numerous occasions, in the past, I have heard different people say that when Jesus said, "It is finished", He was saying that His redemptive sacrifice was finished. For years that is what I believed also.

But, on the contrary, that is not what Jesus meant when He uttered those words. St. Paul tells us that the redemptive sacrifice of Jesus was not finished until He was resurrected from the dead; not at His death on the cross. This means that our redemptive salvation would not be completed until the resurrection of Our Lord on the third day after his death on the cross.

In Chapter 15 of St. Paul's first letter to the Corinthians, he explains that our redemptive salvation would not be complete without the resurrection of Our Lord and Savior, Jesus Christ.

> *But now Christ has been raised from the dead, the first fruits of those who have fallen asleep. For since death came through a human being, the resurrection of the dead came also through a human being. For just as in Adam all die, so too in Christ shall all be brought to life but each one in proper order: Christ the firstfruits; then, at his coming, those who belong to Christ.*
>
> 1Corenthians 15:20-23

So, if His redemptive sacrifice was not finished with His death on the cross, then what was finished? As noted in the brief outline of the Passover meal, the meal consisted of drinking four cups of wine with the fourth cup of wine marking the end of the Passover Meal. But Jesus did not drink the fourth cup of wine in the upper room at the Passover meal. As Our Lord hung on the cross and sucked the sour wine from the sponge on the hyssop branch, it is at that moment that He was consuming the fourth cup of wine to finish and bring to a close, the Passover meal that began in the upper room the night before. He was consuming the fourth cup of wine, *the cup of consummation.*

Through all of my research and analysis, the most revealing and informative discovery for me was the relationship between the Passover celebration and the crucifixion. As I learned from the writings of Dr. Scott Hahn, the meaning of the fourth cup of wine that is consumed during the Passover meal, it all came together for me. I was also reminded that the Passover celebration included the eating of the sacrificial lamb as well as a thanksgiving offering of bread and wine.

A thanksgiving offering has always been a part of the Passover celebration. Centuries before the time of Jesus, again as noted by Dr. Scott Hahn, an ancient Jewish prophet proclaimed that a bread and wine offering would replace the sacrificing of animals in the Temple.

NISAN (Abib) - March/April

Sun	Mon	Tue	Wed	Thu	Fri	Sat
					1	2
3	4	5	6	7	8	9
10 - Sunday	11 - Monday	12 - Tuesday	13 - Wednesday	14 - Thursday	15 - Friday	16 - Saturday
LAMB SELECTION PALM SUNDAY (day one)	Lamb on Display Jesus in Temple (day two)	Lamb on Display Jesus in Temple (day three)	Lamb on Display Jesus in Temple (day four)	Lamb on Display Day of Preparation (day five)	PASSOVER & 1st SABBATH OF UNLEAVENED BREAD CRUCIFIXION (day one)	WEEKLY SABBATH (day two)
17 - Sunday	18 - Monday	19 - Tuesday	20 - Wednesday	21 - Thursday	22 - Friday	23 - Saturday
FIRSTFRUITS RESURRECTION (day three)	(day four)	(day five)	(day six)	2nd SABBATH OF UNLEAVEN BREAD (day seven)		
24	25	26	27	28	29	30

Time markers per day: Midnight — 6am — Noon — 6pm

* Daily lamb offerings, morning and evening.

Developed by Larry Lastrapes

And the Lord said to Moses and Aaron in the land of Egypt This month shall be for you the beginning of months: it shall be the first month of the year for you. Tell all the congregations of Israel that on the tenth day of this month they shall take every man, a lamb according to their fathers' houses ... your lamb shall be without blemish, a male, a year-old ... And you shall keep it until the fourteenth day of this month when the whole assembly of the congregation of Israel shall kill their lambs in the evening. (Exodus 12:1-3, 5-6)

The fourteenth day of the month at evening, is the phase of the Lord: And the fifteenth day of the same month is the solemnity of the unleavened bread of the Lord. Seven days shall you eat unleavened bread. On each of the seven days you shall offer an oblation to the LORD. Then on the seventh day you will have a declared holy day, you shall do no heavy work. (Leviticus 23:5-8)

In my other research on the Passover, I learned that the bread and wine thanksgiving offering that takes place during the Passover celebration is called the ***todah*** and it occurs between the third and fourth cups of wine. The Hebrew translation of *todah* is rendered *eucharistia* or in English, thanksgiving. Actually, the bread and wine offering of Melchizedek was a todah offering for Abraham after he defeated the King of Chedorlaomer and three other kings when he rescued his nephew Lot and set him free.

When the Jewish Temple was destroyed by the Romans in AD 70, the sacrificing of animals in the Jewish Temple came to an abrupt end. Although the animal sacrifices in the Temple came to an abrupt end, the todah offering continues to the present day as the thanksgiving offering in the Catholic Mass. The Catholic Mass is the fulfillment of the prophecy of the ancient Jewish prophet.

DARKNESS COVERED THE LAND

In the previous sections of this chapter, several Bible citations document the crucifixion, death, and resurrection of Jesus. But none of those Bible passages tell us the year that those events occurred. The exact year that Jesus was crucified has been researched and discussed by theologians for centuries and some of them still do not agree on the year of the crucifixion. I am not a theologian and I do not have access to all of the documents that they use but, in my search for answers, I am taking an approach that is a new twist to my personal research on that subject. In my attempt to determine the year of the crucifixion, death, and resurrection of Jesus, I shifted the first phase of my research on this subject from the bible to modern-day scientific technology. One of the areas of my research was the internet where I expected to find a lot of different websites on the subject and that is exactly what I found. Within those websites, I discovered that four different years are considered to be the possible year that Jesus was crucified.

As mentioned earlier, the years of the crucifixion that came up most often were AD 27, AD 30, AD 33, and AD 34. Based on the research and scientific calculations of two Oxford scientists, Colin J. Humphreys, and W. G. Waddington, Jesus was crucified in the year AD 33. These scientists, in their scientific research, concluded that there was a full lunar eclipse of the moon on April 3, AD 33 in the evening after Jesus died on the cross. They used modern-day astronomy technology in conjunction with an Old Testament prophecy and a New Testament confirmation that the prophecy was fulfilled.

At this point, I need to Shift from my scientific research and go back to the Old Testament prophecy. Some 800 years before the actual occurrence of the crucifixion and death of Our Lord, we find that, in the Old Testament, it was prophesied that two things were going to transpire after the crucifixion of the Messiah. The first occurrence was the light of the sun would fail and the second was that the moon would turn to blood.

In the book of Joel in the Old Testament, he prophesied that:

> ***The sun shall be turned to darkness and, the moon to blood,***
> ***before the great and awesome day of the Lord.***
>
> Joel 2:31

Also, in the New Testament, in the book of The Acts of the Apostles, it says that St. Peter reminded his listeners, during his Pentecostal speech, that the prophecy of Joel was fulfilled on the day that Our Lord died.

> ***The sun shall be turned to darkness, and the moon to blood,***
> ***before the day of the Lord comes...***
>
> Acts 2:20

In the scripture passage above (*Acts 2:20*), I want to focus on the first part of that passage; ***"The sun shall be turned to darkness."*** Three of the four gospels in the New Testament, Matthew *(27:45)*, Mark *(15:33)*, and Luke *(23:44)*, state that after Jesus was crucified and raised on the cross, there was darkness for three hours - from the sixth hour until the ninth hour (from about noon to about 3:00 PM). Some bible translations refer to the darkness as an eclipse but an eclipse, as we know it, only lasts a few minutes.

Also, it was the annual Passover celebration and as always, Passover occurs in the middle of the month when it is always a full moon. This is when the crucifixion occurred, in the middle of the month. As you may recall from your junior high or high school science classes that when there is a full moon, the earth is positioned between the sun and the moon. In this alignment of the solar bodies, a solar eclipse of the moon is virtually impossible. A solar eclipse of the moon can only occur when the moon is between the sun and the earth. At the crucifixion of Jesus, the sun, earth, and moon were in the wrong alignment for a solar eclipse to occur.

In the gospel of Luke, which is originally written in Greek, the Greek words *"heliou eklipontos"* are used to describe the darkening of the sky during the crucifixion. The exact translation of those words renders the following meaning:

Heliou = *the sun*

Eklipontos = *a participle of the verb ekleipō, which means "fail/leave off/cease, to fail or leave, to come to an end, off or cease.*

These same Greek words, which mean that the light of the sun has failed, are used to describe a regular solar eclipse also.

As I tried to understand, in more detail, the phenomenon of the darkness during the crucifixion of Jesus, I turned my attention back to the internet once again. To my amazement, I made two very important discoveries. First, in ancient Greece, they used the Olympiads and the number of years that an emperor was on the throne as the standard method of ancient historical dating of events. Secondly, I discovered that the darkness phenomenon was documented by several secular (non-religious) writers. The secular documentation that grabbed my attention was the one by the Greek historian Phlegon. In AD 137 he wrote about the darkness phenomenon in his document titled, "History of the Olympiads". In that document, he stated the following:

In the fourth year of the 202nd Olympiad, there was an eclipse of the Sun which was greater than any known before and in the sixth hour of the day it became night; so that stars appeared in the heaven, and a great Earthquake that broke out in Bithynia destroyed the greatest part of Nicaea.

After reading this quotation, I felt that I needed to understand the role of the Olympiads in dating ancient events. At this point, my research took another turn as I re-directed my focus on the ancient Olympics. I discovered that the word "Olympiad" is a Greek term that represents a time period of four years. Although the ancient games of the Olympics occurred every four years, each year of an Olympiad is a reference to an actual calendar year. The first ancient Olympiad took place in the year 776 BC. When counting the Olympiad years, the first year of the first Olympiad was 776 BC, the second year of the first Olympiad was 775 BC, etc.

The beginning of the four-year ancient Olympiad period always began on July 1st and ended on June 30th four years later. The ancient Olympic Games always occurred in the first week of the first year of the Olympiad. Just a side note - the first Olympic game only lasted one day and it consisted of one event - a long-distance run. By comparison, our modern-day Olympiad always begins on January 1st and ends on December 31st four years later. Our modern-day Olympic games occur during the summer of the first year of the Olympiad.

Looking back at the writing of Phlegon where he talks about the darkening phenomenon, he states that the darkness occurred in the 4th year of the 202nd Olympiad. It is documented that the 202nd Olympiad began in AD 29 and the fourth year of the 202nd Olympiad would be AD 33. Phlegon's document also states that:

> *...in the time of Tiberius Caesar, at full moon, there was a full eclipse of the sun from the 6th hour to the 9th hour.*

His documented time of the darkness matches the time documented in the gospels of Matthew, Mark, and Luke. Note that his quotation says that there was a *"full moon"* and at the same time there was a *"full eclipse of the sun"*. Looking back at the Greek words for an eclipse, Phlegon was saying that the ***"light of the*** *sun failed"*. The other point in Phlegon's quotation that caught my attention was the phrase, *"...it became night; so that stars appeared in the heaven;"* This description tells me that this darkness was very different from any eclipse as we know them. With a typical eclipse when the moon passes between the sun and the earth, the darkness is localized in a relatively small area and total darkness is not experienced.

The light of the sun failed completely during the crucifixion and total darkness was experienced. According to the three gospels (Matthew, Mark, and Luke), this darkness covered the entire world, which at that time, was the Mediterranean region. Some ancient writings even suggest that the darkness covered the entire earth.

With the writings of the three Gospel writers and the Olympiad historical writer Phlegon, I think it is safe to conclude that the darkness phenomenon is well documented as an actual occurrence. Phlegon states that the darkness occurred in the year AD 33 but he does not say when it happened in that year. The gospel writers state that there was darkness during the crucifixion and we know that Jesus was crucified in the Jewish month of Nisan during the annual celebration of the Feast of Unleavened Bread which always occurred in the middle of the month of Nisan.

The Moon Shall Turn to Blood

In addition to the darkness that lasted for three hours while our Lord hung on the cross, the second part of the Old Testament prophecy of Joel was fulfilled also. The second part of the prophecy states that *"...the moon would turn to blood before the great and awesome day of the Lord."* As mentioned before, St. Peter reminded everyone that the prophecy of Joel was fulfilled on the day that Jesus was crucified. In addition to the New Testament documents the crucifixion of Jesus at the annual Passover in the Jewish month of Nisan, it is also documented as an astronomy phenomenon.

Now, to understand how and why the moon turned to blood, I needed to look at the secular documentation of a blood moon. I was looking for concurrence with the Gospel writers that it really occurred in the evening after Jesus died. I turned my attention to another secular documentation that is considered to be the most accurate scientific data on eclipses, the National Aeronautics and Space Administration (NASA) "JavaScript Solar Eclipse Explorer". The NASA JavaScript states the following:

> *As the earth rotates on its axis, tidal friction is imposed on it through the gravitational attraction with the moon and, to a lesser extent, the sun. This secular acceleration gradually transfers angular momentum from earth to the moon.*

Wow! What in the world does that mean? To simplify that somewhat confusing scientific statement, it is saying that the orbits of the earth and moon are constantly changing. In the scientific world, this constantly changing phenomenon of the orbits of the earth and the moon is commonly referred to as delta-T. Delta-T is a mathematical formula that is used to look at the exact position of astronomy bodies at a specific time in the past or in the future.

The delta-T formula was developed by F. R. Stephenson and L. V. Morrison and published in AD 1984. It shows that the moon is gradually drifting away from the earth (about 1.6" per year) while the rotation of the earth is gradually slowing (about 40 seconds per century). With this valuable knowledge, the delta-T formula can be used to go back to the year AD 33 and show the exact alignment of the sun, earth, and moon. It is a formula that enables the scientist to track the exact position of the earth and the moon at a specific time in the past or the future.

Initially, computer technology that was used to go back in time did not include the delta-T formula. Without the delta-T formula, computer programs that produced astronomy data of past events were not totally accurate. The two non-religious Oxford scholars mentioned earlier, Colin J. Humphreys and W. G. Waddington, used modern-day astronomy technology in conjunction with the delta-T formula to go back in time and research the year that Jesus was crucified. Their findings were published in the British journal *Nature* where they stated that the crucifixion of Jesus took place on a Friday in April in the year AD 33 (Julian calendar). They confirmed that a blood moon was visible in Jerusalem in the evening after Jesus died. For centuries scholars agreed that there was a blood moon in the evening after Jesus died but they did not believe that it could be seen from Jerusalem. With the advent of the delta-T formula, the Oxford scholars, Humphreys and Waddington, in their publications, contradicted the ancient scholars when they stated that the blood moon was visible from Jerusalem. It was the delta-T formula that showed the correct alignment of the earth and moon that enabled the Oxford scholars to conclude that the blood moon was visible from Jerusalem. And in total agreement with the Gospels, our modern-day scientists concur that a blood moon was visible in Jerusalem after Jesus died.

With all of this background and documentation on the occurrence of a blood moon in the evening after Jesus died, I found myself in a peculiar position. I did not know anything about a blood moon. Actually, I did not really think that it was an actual astronomy occurrence because I had never seen one. Now I find myself in a position where I needed to be educated on still another scientific phenomenon that was documented scientifically and in the Bible.

Once again the internet came to my rescue in a NASA publication on blood moons. First of all, I learned that a blood moon is an actual astronomy phenomenon and they really do occur. According to NASA, regarding the occurrence of blood moons, *"two to four per year and each one is visible over about half the earth."* It happens when the moon is full and the earth is between the moon and the sun. A blood moon occurs during a full moon as it passes through the darkest shadow of the earth. In some cases a blood moon can last more than thirty minutes but, according to NASA data, the blood moon that occurred on the night after Jesus died was visible in Jerusalem for about twelve minutes and thirty seconds.

Understanding why the moon looks blood-red during a full lunar eclipse requires an analysis of the light rays of the sun. The light from the sun is white just like the white light we see from a regular flashlight. Without getting too scientific, the white light of the sun is made up of a spectrum of seven basic colors: violet, indigo, blue, green, yellow, orange, and red. Each light ray has a different wavelength which is what causes them to be different colors.

The different wavelengths of the light rays react differently when they enter the atmosphere surrounding the earth. The blue light rays are the shortest ones and they cannot fully penetrate the earth's atmosphere. Since they cannot fully penetrate the atmosphere of the earth they bounce off of the atmosphere that surrounds the earth and are refracted back into the void of space. When we look up at the sky during the day, the blue sky that we see is the refracted blue light rays that are bouncing off of the atmosphere that surrounds the earth.

More of the medium-length and long-length light rays can penetrate the atmosphere but they are refracted or bend differently and cause the earth to cast two types of shadows. The refraction of the medium-length light rays causes the earth to cast a light shadow that is called the penumbra (see the Blood Moon diagram). The longest light rays, the red ones, when refracted through the earth's atmosphere causes the earth to cast a dark shadow that is called the umbra.

As we all know, the earth orbits the sun and the moon orbits the earth. The orbital plane of the earth around the sun is not the same as the orbital plane of the moon around the earth. The difference between the orbital planes of the earth and the moon is about 5 degrees. Basically, this means that the earth and moon are not in the same orbital plane and, consequently, the moon does not pass through the dark shadow of the earth very often. A lunar eclipse will happen only when the earth is perfectly aligned between the moon and the sun and the moon passes through the dark shadow of the earth. With all of that being said, this brings us to the blood moon phenomenon.

As mentioned, the earth has two shadows from the sun, the penumbra, and the umbra. The penumbra shadow is lighter and the larger of the two shadows while the umbra or the smaller shadow which is darker and is made from the red light rays that are refracted through the earth's atmosphere. A blood moon will occur during a full lunar eclipse when the moon passes through the umbra or the red-refracted light rays of the earth.

So, as the moon passes through the umbra shadow of the earth, the red light rays are reflected off of the surface of the moon. This is a normal astronomy occurrence that happens, per NASA, about three or four times per year.

The NASA data confirms that there was a full lunar eclipse and a blood moon on the night after Jesus died on the cross. Although this is a normal astronomy occurrence, the Old Testament prophecy of the moon turning to blood was made some 800 years before Jesus was crucified. In the Old Testament Book of Joel, it states that the "***moon will turn to blood before the day of the Lord.***"

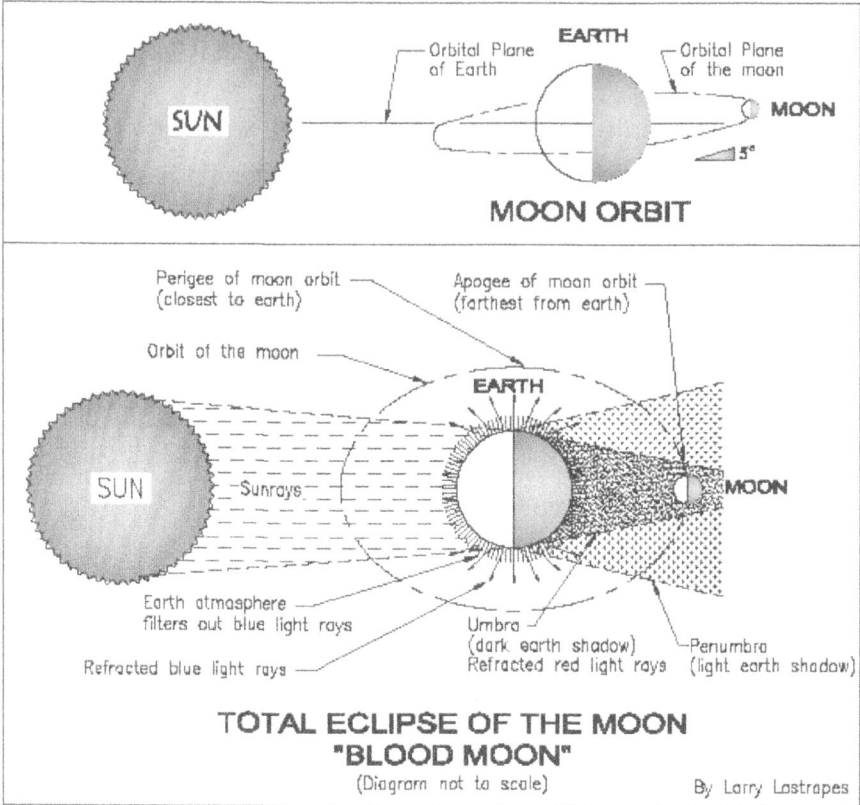

MOON ORBIT

Labels in diagram:
- EARTH
- Orbital Plane of Earth
- Orbital Plane of the moon
- SUN
- MOON
- 5°

TOTAL ECLIPSE OF THE MOON
"BLOOD MOON"
(Diagram not to scale)   By Larry Lastrapes

Labels in diagram:
- Perigee of moon orbit (closest to earth)
- Apogee of moon orbit (farthest from earth)
- Orbit of the moon
- EARTH
- SUN
- Sunrays
- MOON
- Earth atmosphere filters out blue light rays
- Refracted blue light rays
- Umbra (dark earth shadow) Refracted red light rays
- Penumbra (light earth shadow)

After reading this scripture quote several times, I found myself questioning the meaning of the phrase *"day of the Lord."* As I researched numerous websites on the internet in an attempt to gain some insight into the meaning of the phrase, I made another interesting discovery. I learned that the phrase is not a reference to a specific calendar date or time but, instead, it is a reference to an event.

Whenever this phrase is used in the Old Testament or the New Testament it has to be viewed in the context of the writing. In the Old Testament book of Joel, the *"day of the Lord"* phrase was prophesying the coming of the Messiah. We know this because it is confirmed in the book of the Acts of the Apostles *(Acts 2:20)*, in the New Testament. St. Peter confirms that the context of the prophecy of Joel was about the death of Jesus.

After comparing the Bible documentation with the scientific documentation, I believe that Jesus was crucified and died on April 3 in the year AD 33. I also concluded, with confidence, that there was total darkness for three hours while Jesus hung on the cross and there was a blood moon in the evening after he died.

CHAPTER 6

ADAM AND EVE, ORIGINAL SIN, AND THE RESURRECTION

A s my knowledge of Holy Week was broadened through my research I felt a need to learn more. I needed to know more about Adam and Eve, original sin, and how they were impacted by the resurrection. In my ongoing research, I discovered that there was so much more to each of those topics than I ever imagined. Adam and Eve are more than just the first two humans created by God. The consequences of original sin are totally different from anything that ever crossed my mind. Additionally, through these new discoveries, I gained a better understanding of the meaning of God's grace.

ADAM AND EVE

As I sat in my home library one evening thinking about some of the things that I had just learned about Adam and Eve, I noticed a book on a bookshelf. I retrieved it and discovered that it was a book that I purchased several years earlier but I never spent any quality time reading or studying it. Taking a closer look at the title and some of its content, I saw that the book title was "Catholic Bible Dictionary" and it was published in 2009 with Dr. Scott Hahn as the general editor.

I opened the book, decided to look up Adam, and made an amazing discovery. I discovered that this book was validating some of the things that I read on the internet about Adam and Eve. It explained that they were more than just the first humans created by God. In addition to dwelling in Paradise in the presence of God, they had a share in the divine nature of God which elevated them to a supernatural order, made them holy, and put them in divine communion with God.

They were created as perfect supernatural beings, without sin, and they dwelled and walked with God in Paradise. In addition to dwelling in Paradise, also called the Garden of Eden, God gave Adam dominion over the entire earth and every creature on the planet.

And God blessed them and God said to them, "Be fruitful and multiply, and fill the earth and subdue it; and have dominion over the fish of the sea and over the birds of the air and over every living thing that moves upon the earth."

Genesis 1:28

I have read this passage numerous times but I never paid much attention to the word dominion, until now. I decided to look up the definition in Google. Google defines dominion in biblical terms as "the right to dominate and to possess absolute control over the entire earth." So, by definition, dominion means absolute power. By definition, the word dominion means absolute power. Recall that the bible tells us that God created Adam in His divine image *(Genesis 1:26)*. Dr. Scott Hahn noted that in Near Eastern literature the "image" motif is associated with kings. Adam was the ruler of his kingdom, the entire earth and he was in full control and ruled over everything. Like any other ruler of a kingdom, he was a king and Eve was his queen. In other words, Adam and Eve were royalty.

As a supernatural being living in Paradise with God, Adam had a covenantal relationship with God. In this relationship with God his loyalty and trust were of the utmost importance. Adam and Eve were created by God as perfect beings to live in Paradise for all of eternity. It goes without saying that their descendants were destined to dwell in Paradise with them for all of eternity. With all of this power and authority, he did not report to anyone except God.

In addition to their supernatural state and his dominion over the entire earth, God also gave Adam and Eve a free will. They had total freedom to do anything they wanted to do but they would be held fully accountable for all of their choices, good or bad. Within their dwelling place, the Garden of Eden, God gave them one small caveat; they could not eat the fruit of the tree in the middle of the Garden or even touch it. When God placed Adam in the Garden of Eden He told him the rule in the Garden regarding the tree and the consequences if the rule was broken.

> *And the Lord God commanded the man, saying, "You may freely eat of every tree of the garden; but the tree of the knowledge of good and evil you shall not eat, for in the day that you eat of it you shall die."*
>
> Genesis 2:16-17

In the vocabulary section before Chapter One, the word concupiscence is defined. Although Adam and Eve were created without sin, elevated to a supernatural order with a share in the divine nature of God, they were not immune from concupiscence. They still had the freedom of choice. When they ate the fruit from the tree in the garden, they were exercising their free will. But the choice that they made was more than an act of disobedience; it was a breach of the binding loyalty and trust they had in their covenantal agreement with God. The consequences of their breach of loyalty and trust resulted in the loss of the state of their supernatural order, their holiness, and their divine communion with God.

THE GRACE OF GOD

The grace of God is a supernatural gift or favor that is given to rational beings; angels and humans. It cannot be earned; it is a supernatural gift from God. A natural human is not capable of earning anything that is on a supernatural level. There are two types of supernatural gifts that God gives us; actual grace and sanctifying Grace.

Although both types of graces are supernatural gifts from God and sound very much alike, they are very different. Actual grace is external to the soul and sanctifying grace is internal, acts directly upon the soul, dwells within, and gives the soul supernatural life.

One of the many ways that God communicates with us regularly is through actual grace. Every day each one of us will find ourselves in a situation where we may be tempted to do something questionable. After thinking about the temptation, we may think that "I can't do that because it would be wrong?" That thought process is the working of actual grace giving you a supernatural nudge. Whenever we are tempted to commit a sinful act and we realize that our pending behavior is sinful or wrong, that realization of that pending behavior is the working of actual grace.

Actual grace is a supernatural push or a form of encouragement from God that acts upon our will and intellect. It acts on us in such a way that if we follow through with that behavior it would be a sinful act. Although actual grace acts on the soul externally it never affects or alters our free will. It does not live in the soul and transform it like sanctifying grace. With our free will, we can still choose to listen to that supernatural kick in the pants or we can ignore it and sin by knowingly committing an act that goes against the will of God.

Sanctifying grace is totally different from actual grace. With the supernatural gift of Sanctifying Grace, the human soul is transformed and elevated to a supernatural order, making it holy and giving it a share in the divine nature of God. Sharing in the divine nature of God puts us in divine communion with God. As stated on the Catholic Answers website, Sanctifying Grace *is* a supernatural life. It was this grace or supernatural gift from God that elevated Adam and Eve to a supernatural order, made them holy, and placed them in divine communion with God.

As I was reading about sanctifying grace and how it transforms the soul, I noticed the word "infused" in the Catholic Answers article on Sanctifying grace. I have read this article several times but that word never caught my attention before. After the word finally caught my attention I decided to look it up on the Catholic Answers website to see if I could get a better understanding of the usage in that context.

Amazingly I discovered from the website that the ancient Catholic theologians referred to Sanctifying Grace as "Infused Grace". They used that description of sanctifying grace because the bible says that grace was poured into the soul.

> *...he saved us, not because of deeds done by us in righteousness, but in virtue of his own mercy, by the washing of regeneration and renewal in the Holy Spirit, which he poured out upon us richly through Jesus Christ our Savior, so that we might be justified by his grace and become heirs in hope of eternal life.*
>
> Titus 3:5-7

Only beings that are infused with the supernatural gift of Sanctifying Grace are transformed to be like Adam and Eve were. The infusion of sanctifying grace in the soul makes it possible for them to dwell in the presence of God. Additionally, like Adam and Eve, a soul that is infused with sanctifying grace will be elevated to a supernatural order, made holy, and given a share in the divinity of God thereby placing them in divine communion with God.

The soul of a rational being that has been transformed by the infusion of sanctifying grace is fully alive. By contrast, a soul without sanctifying grace is separated from God which makes it spiritually dead. When God told Adam, regarding the eating of the fruit of the tree in the Garden of Eden, *"...for in the day that you eat of it you shall die" (Genesis 2:17),* He was telling him that if they ate the fruit from the tree in the middle of the garden the supernatural gift of sanctifying grace would be taken from them and they would be rendered spiritually dead. Again, a soul without sanctifying grace is separated from God which makes that soul spiritually dead.

ORIGINAL SIN

From the early years of my childhood, I was taught that all humans are descendants of Adam and Eve, and this teaching is also confirmed in the Bible. While I have truly believed this teaching from my childhood and into my adult life, I had a difficult time understanding why or how we, the descendants of Adam and Eve inherited their sinful breach of loyalty and trust that we call original sin. In my search for an answer to this question, more questions ran through my mind. I concluded that I needed a more in-depth understanding of the meaning of original sin.

After several weeks of reading numerous internet websites on the subject of original sin, I concluded that the most informative explanation for me was on the "Catholic Answers" website. The website states that we are not responsible for the sinful act of Adam and Eve and we did not inherit the sin itself. The article goes on to tell us that we inherited the stain of Original sin. As noted in The Catholic Answers article on Original Sin, the primary consequence of Original Sin resulted in a chain reaction of consequences.

> *As death is the privation of the principle of life, the death of the soul is the privation of sanctifying grace which, according to all theologians, is the principle of supernatural life.*
>
> Catholic Answers, "Nature of Original Sin"

In other words, if Adam and Eve had not sinned they never would have experienced death. They would have lived in Paradise for all of eternity in the presence of God as supernatural beings ruling the entire earth. That also means that all of us humans who are the descendants of Adam and Eve would have inherited their supernatural order and lived in Paradise for all of eternity.

Sadly, Adam and Eve sinned and the consequences of that first sin, also called Original Sin or the fall, caused the *"privation of sanctifying grace"* to themselves and their descendants. The side effect or the stain caused by the privation of sanctifying grace is the inheritance that the descendants of Adam and Eve received.

In the Catholic Encyclopedia section of the Catholic Answers website it states that the Council of Trent authorized the following explanation of Original Sin:

> *...Original sin is the death of the soul and a privation of justice that each child contracts at its conception.*
>
> *...Therefore the absence of sanctifying grace in a child is a real privation; it is the want of something that should have been in him according to the Divine plan.*
>
> *...Consequently the privation of this grace, even without any other act, would be a stain, a moral deformity, a turning away from,*
>
> *...This privation, therefore, is the hereditary stain.*

After going through all of this research on Adam and Eve, it occurred to me that the worst part of the sin of Adam and Eve was not their eating of the forbidden fruit; it was the violation of the covenantal agreement that they had with God. In addition to the breach of their sacred agreement with God, Satan convinced Adam that he would gain more power than he already had and be like a god if he ate the fruit from the tree in the middle of the Garden of Eden. That made the breach of his covenantal agreement even more serious.

But the snake said to the woman "You certainly will not die! God knows well that when you eat of it your eyes will be opened and you will be like gods, who know good and evil."

...and she also gave some to her husband, who was with her, and he ate it.

Genesis 3:4-5, 6

When Adam and Eve sinned and lost the state of their supernatural order, holiness, and divine communion with God, they were cast out of Paradise and the gates to Paradise were closed to them and all of their descendants. Adam and Eve became normal humans and that new status was passed on to their descendants.

Neither Adam, Eve nor their descendants, as normal humans, could atone for their sin and the breach of their covenantal agreement with God. Because they were supernatural beings without sin when they committed their covenantal breach, the atonement for their sin could only be accomplished by a supernatural being without sin. Jesus is the supernatural being in a supernatural state and without sin who came and paid the ransom for the sin of Adam and Eve. The ransom price that Jesus had to pay for the sin of Adam and Eve was His death on the cross followed by His resurrection.

Before we can dwell in heaven with God, the Divine honor that Adam and Eve possessed had to be restored and the Divine wrath of God had to be appeased.

Adam and Eve and all of mankind existed under a veil of servitude to sin and evil. The first and original sin of Adam and Eve had to be ransomed before any of their descendants could be admitted into Paradise. Only a perfect Divine being in a supernatural state and without sin could remove the veil of servitude. The redemptive deliverance of all humans

was necessary for the restoration of mankind's original re-
lationship with God.

EWTN and The Catechism of the Catholic Church – Part. 3,
section 1, chapter 1, article 1

The hereditary stain of Original Sin was passed on to the descendants of Adam and Eve and at birth, every human will experience the privation of sanctifying grace. Without sanctifying grace a person will not experience the Divine Honor and supernatural relationship with God that Adam and Eve had before they sinned. It is through baptism and calling on the Holy Spirit that the hereditary stain of original sin is washed away and sanctifying grace is infused into the soul.

After baptism, no one runs the risk of having sanctifying grace taken away before they reach the age of reasoning. Reaching the age of reason means that an individual has a clear understanding of what is right and what is wrong. If a person commits a deadly sin after reaching the age of reason they will experience the privation of sanctifying grace that existed in them before they were baptized. In this situation they must repent of their sin and be reconciled with God before sanctifying grace is infused back into their soul by God. The process of reconciliation was instituted by Jesus after his resurrection when He gave the apostles the authority to forgive sins through confession. It is through the confessing of our sins that we are forgiven for our sins and confession is the atonement that makes us "at one" with God.

Jesus said to them again, "As the Father has sent me, even so, I
send you." And when He had said this, He breathed on them,
and said to them, "Receive the Holy Spirit. If you forgive the
sins of any, they are forgiven; if you retain the sins of any,
they are retained."

John 20:21-23

In this section it was explained that committing a deadly sin will result in the loss of sanctifying grace. And, as noted, without sanctifying grace the human soul is spiritually dead and cannot dwell in the presence of God. With the Ten Commandment as a starting point, a few examples of deadly or mortal sins would include murder, stealing, adultery, fornication; lust, hatred and idolatry just to name a few.

THE RESURRECTION OF JESUS

I have always heard that Jesus died for our sins and I have always believed and accepted that teaching. But I also had to be honest with myself and acknowledge that I did not understand the full meaning of that teaching. Unlike the secular documentation of the sky turning dark for three hours during the crucifixion and the blood moon in the evening after the death of Jesus, there is no secular documentation that validates the religious teachings of the resurrection of Jesus. The books of the New Testament and the traditional teachings of the apostles are the only sources we have that attest to the resurrection of Jesus.

The death and resurrection of Our Lord was the culmination of the Jubilee year that He inaugurated in the synagogue in the final year of His public ministry. Please note that, as mentioned earlier, our redemptive salvation was not complete with only the death of Jesus. His resurrection was totally necessary to complete His mission of redemption.

While the gates of Heaven were closed from the time of the original sin of Adam and Eve, all of the ancient souls of the righteous awaited the Redeemer. They existed in a place that the Old Testament called Sheol which denotes the underworld of the dead.

> *...Jesus did not descend into hell to deliver the damned, nor to destroy the hell of damnation, but to free the just who had gone before him.*
>
> Catechism of the Catholic Church, Chapter 2, Article 5, Paragraph 633

> *...The hour is coming when all who are in the tombs will hear his voice and come forth, those who have done good, to*

the resurrection of life, and those who have done evil, to the resurrection of judgment.

John 5:28-29

In addition to the ancient practice of offering the first fruits of the barley harvest back to God on the Sunday after the Saturday Passover during the Feast of Unleavened Bread, the ancients also celebrated the Jubilee year by forgiving debts, freeing slaves, and returning property to the original owners. These practices of the Jubilee year were a foreshadowing of our redemptive salvation that would be accomplished through the death and resurrection of Jesus. The offering of the first fruits signaled the beginning of the agricultural harvest. In the resurrection, Jesus was the first to be resurrected or the first fruit of the spiritual harvest. After His resurrection, all of mankind was redeemed from their veil of servitude to sin and evil which enabled them to be resurrected. The gospel of Matthew tells us that after the resurrection of Jesus, many of those who had died came out of their tombs and were seen by many in the city.

...Tombs were opened, and the bodies of many saints who had fallen asleep were raised. And coming forth from their tombs after his resurrection, they entered the holy city and appeared to many.

Matthew 27:52-53

It was the resurrection of Our Lord in conjunction with his death on the cross that completed our redemptive salvation. The gates of heaven were re-opened and the promises of the Jubilee Year were fulfilled as each one of us was set free from our servitude to sin and evil. So, through the death and resurrection of Jesus, we have all been redeemed!

ONCE FOR ALL

The Bible tells us that Jesus died and was resurrected once for everyone. At first glance, the Bible passage below seems to be telling us that the death and resurrection of Jesus forgave all sins – past, present, and future.

> *For by a single offering he has perfected for all time those who are sanctified*.
>
> Hebrews 10:14

As I mentioned earlier in this chapter in the section on Adam and Eve; they were created as perfect supernatural beings, without sin; they dwelled and walked with God in Paradise. The supernatural gift from God that permitted them to dwell with Him in Paradise was Sanctifying Grace. When they sinned in the Garden of Eden they experienced a *"privation of sanctifying grace"*. Without sanctifying grace no rational being can dwell in the presence of God.

After their sin, Adam and Eve became normal humans without the supernatural gift of sanctifying grace from God. Without sanctifying grace their entire existence changed and they lived in a state of bondage or servitude to sin. Since this condition was caused by their transgression as supernatural humans, they could not reverse this condition because they were changed by their sin and became normal humans. Only a supernatural human is capable of paying the price of redemption for a transgression that is committed by a supernatural being. As mentioned earlier, Jesus is the supernatural being who redeemed all of mankind from slavery and the bondage of sin and restored the whole process of regaining supernatural life or sanctifying grace.

The death and resurrection of Jesus paid the ransom for all sins and regained sanctifying grace for all of mankind. It is important to note that our sins were forgiven and sanctifying grace was regained but it is still possible to experience a privation of sanctifying grace if we commit a deadly or mortal sin. When we say that we are redeemed we are saying that Jesus made it possible for sanctifying grace to be restored within us if we lost it by committing a deadly sin. It does not mean that any sin that we commit will be overlooked by God and forgiven automatically.

Jesus made it very clear that everyone will be held accountable for their sins. When we sin we offend God and we separate ourselves from Him. We must reconcile or restore our relationship with God before we can dwell with Him in heaven. We learned this directly from Jesus himself when he taught us to pray the Lord's Prayer in the Gospel of Matthew. He taught us that we must ask God to forgive our sins and he goes on to tell us that God will forgive us and restore our relationship with Him only if we forgive anyone who has offended us.

This teaching from Jesus was given to us in the Lord's Prayer before his death and resurrection. After His death and resurrection, he told us what we needed to do for our sins to be forgiven.

> *...And forgive us our trespasses as we forgive those who tres-pass against us;*
>
> *...For if you forgive men their trespasses, your heavenly Fa-ther also will forgive you; but if you do not forgive men their trespasses, neither will your Father forgive your trespasses.*
>
> Matthew 6:12, 14

I have seen the scripture passage that tells us that Jesus died for our sins and I have always accepted that teaching. Then I decided that I needed to understand why I had to confess my sins. As I studied the message of the Lord's Prayer, I learned that Jesus Himself was telling us in that prayer, as noted above, that we must ask God the Father for forgiveness for any sin that we commit. Then I learned from the letter to the Hebrews in the New Testament that we will face judgment and punishment for our sins if we do not ask God the Father to forgive us. That scripture passage in the letter to the Hebrews makes it clear that we will be held accountable for sins that are committed after gaining knowledge of the truth.

> *For if we sin deliberately after receiving the knowledge of the truth, there no longer remains a sacrifice for sins, but a fearful prospect of judgment, and a fury of fire that will consume the adversaries.*
>
> Hebrews 10:26-27

Before His death and resurrection, Jesus told us that we had to ask for forgiveness for our sins because our sinful acts, past or future will not be forgiven automatically. Just in case we might be thinking that this teaching does not apply because it was given to us before Our Lord's death and resurrection, He reinforced the teaching after His death and resurrection and before his ascension. He gave the apostles and their successors the power to forgive or not to forgive sins.

If we think about this authority that was given to the apostles by Jesus, a sin would have to be committed and confessed before a decision to forgive or not to forgive the sin can be made. In other words, forgiveness of our sins and confession go hand-in-hand.

> *Jesus said to them again, "Peace be with you. As the Father has sent me, even so, I send you." And when He said this, he breathed on them and said to them, "Receive the Holy Spirit. If you forgive the sins of any they are forgiven. If you retain the sins of any, they are retained."*
>
> John 20:21-23

With the death and resurrection of Jesus, the sin of Adam and Eve and all sins were ransomed and we were redeemed. Jesus, through His redemptive death and resurrection, made it possible for the privation of sanctifying grace to be restored within us. As mentioned earlier, we will experience a privation of sanctifying grace whenever a deadly or mortal sin has been committed. We must repent of our sins through confession and return to following the teachings of God. It is also important to note that the death and resurrection of Jesus caused the gates of Paradise to be opened and never to close again. No sin committed by anyone can cause the gates of Paradise to be closed to everyone. The gates of Paradise will only be closed to the individual sinner who refuses to repent.

Before the death and resurrection of Jesus, the Israelites offered two lambs in the Temple every day. This was an instruction given to the Israelites through Moses. The first lamb was a burnt offering in the morning for redemption, the forgiveness of sins, the coming of the Messiah, and the resurrection of the dead together with other offerings that were being placed on the burning lamb. In the evening (about midafternoon) the second lamb was placed on top of the first burning lamb and sandwiched all of the offerings of the day between the two burning lambs. The offerings continued to burn throughout the night and the process was repeated the next day.

The burnt offerings had to be made every day because the animals are not supernatural or perfect. Conversely, Jesus is supernatural and perfect. He is the sacrificial lamb given to us by God. He is the sacrificial lamb, the Lamb of God. With His redemptive death and resurrection, Jesus died once for all ransoming our sins and making it possible for the restoration of sanctifying grace through confession and repentance for our sins.

CHAPTER 7

A SECOND REVELATION

As noted earlier in Chapter 4, in the section titled "Jesus Enters Jerusalem," Ezekiel had a vision of the Messiah entering the temple area through the East Gate. Ezekiel also received a second supernatural vision and revelation concerning the return of the Messiah. His vision revealed that the East gate in the wall surrounding Jerusalem would be closed until the return of the Messiah.

THE RETURN OF THE MESSIAH

Personally, I have never been to Jerusalem or on a tour of the Holy Land. I spoke with my brother-in-law after he toured the Holy Land and he was curious about the East Gate being sealed. Additionally, he did not understand why there was a cemetery outside of the East Gate. I was able to share with him the results of my research on the current status of Jerusalem. I told him that, in 1517, the Turks conquered and took full control of Jerusalem and the areas surrounding the Jerusalem walls.

As Jesus prophesied in the New Testament, Jerusalem was conquered by the Romans in AD 70, and, among other things; the Jewish Temple located on the Temple Mount was destroyed. Early in the 7th century, under the leadership of Caliph Umar who was a close companion of the prophet Muhammad, the Muslims were able to gain control of Jerusalem. They constructed the Dome of the Rock and Al-Aqsa Mosque on the site of the old Jewish Temple located on the Temple Mount. Over the centuries that ensued, several severe earthquakes destroyed the Dome and the Mosque, and each time they were reconstructed.

At the end of the 11th century, the Christian Crusaders captured Jerusalem but only retained control for one century as the Muslims regained control of Jerusalem at the end of the 12th century. Control of this area has changed numerous times over the centuries and today the Old City of Jerusalem is under Israeli control but the mosque is under the administrative control of the Jordanian/Palestinian-led Islamic Waqf.

Although the Muslims do not believe that Jesus is the Messiah, they are familiar with the Old Testament prophecy that the Messiah will return through the East Gate. They wanted to do whatever they could to prevent the return of Jesus so they sealed the East Gate in the Jerusalem wall with structural stones. As an added measure, just in case that does not work, they reinforced their attempt to prevent the return of Jesus by placing a cemetery in front of the sealed East Gate.

They believe that no Holy Man, especially a Messiah, will defile himself by walking through a cemetery. With that mindset, they believe that the Messiah will not return as long as the East Gate remains sealed and the cemetery remains in place. But the second vision of Ezekiel tells a different story.

> *Then he brought me back to the outer gate of the sanctuary facing east, but it was closed . . . he must enter through the vestibule of the gate and leave the same way.*
>
> Ezekiel 44:1, 3

This prophecy is telling us that the east gate will be sealed but the Messiah will still return through the East Gate. At the appointed time in God's plan, the stones that seal the East Gate will be removed and the Messiah, on His return, will enter the Temple area through the East Gate.

APPENDIX 1

ART AND ILLUSTRATIONS

PAGE	TITLE	ARTIST	YEAR
Cover	Triumphal Entry - Maesta	Duccio Di Buoninsegna	1311
--	Icon of Jesus	Larry Lastrapes	2018
6	Journey of Abraham	Larry Lastrapes	2018
21	Map – Herodian Tetrarchy	Larry Lastrapes	2018
46	One-Day Jewish Calendar	Larry Lastrapes	2018
51	One-Year Jewish Calendar	Larry Lastrapes	2018
64	Tower of the Flock	Photographer unknown	1920
70	Reconstruction of Mount	Paul Volz	1914
82	Map – Final Journey	Larry Lastrapes	2018
97	Triumphal Entry	Pietro Lorenzetti	1320
113	Map – Jerusalem Walls	Larry Lastrapes	2018
114	Map – 3D Jerusalem	Larry Lastrapes	2018
119	Nisan Month Calendar	Larry Lastrapes	2017
130	The Blood Moon	Larry Lastrapes	2017

BIBLIOGRAPHY OF CONTRIBUTING RESOURCES

1. **Douay-Rheims Bible**
   http://www.drbo.org/

   This version of the Bible was used to reference a more literal English translation of the Holy Scriptures.

2. **Douay-Rheims Haydock Commentary**
   Rev. George Leo Haydock

   Old and New Testament Commentary used.

3. **The Didache Bible – RSV: With commentaries based on the Catechism of the Catholic Church – Ignatius Bible Edition; Midwest Theological Forum – Ignatius Press.**

   Maps, commentaries, and Apologetical Explanations were used.

4. **Ignatius Catholic Study Bible: New Testament - RSV: Second Catholic Edition - Ignatius Press 2010**

Modern English language, commentaries, and maps were used.

5. **New American Bible, Revised Edition (NABRE), United States Conference of Catholic Bishops**
   http://www.usccb.org/bible/books-of-the-bible/index.cfm

Modern English language and footnote references are used.

6. **A Catholic Commentary on Holy Scripture – Thomas Nelson and Sons Publisher – 1953.**

Scriptural commentaries were used.

7. **New Advent Catholic Encyclopedia**
   http://www.newadvent.org/

Definitions and Commentaries used.

8. **The Catechism Explained - *An Exhaustive Explanation of the Catholic Religion – Fr. Francis Sparigo - The Bellarmine Forum Edition***
   https://bellarmineforum.org

The Promise of The Redeemer section was used.

9. **The Lamb's Supper – The Mass as Heaven on Earth –Dr. Scott Hahn**

Paschal meal. Last Supper and Crucifixion

10. **Eternal Word Television Network (EWTN)**
    http://www.ewtn.com

The Resurrection of the Body

11. **The Complete Works of Flavius Josephus**
    http://www.ultimatebiblereferencelibrary.com

    Jewish religion and cultural norms.

12. **Agape Catholic Bible Study**
    http://www.agapebiblestudy.com

    The Passion Feast

13. **Bible Searchers – Destination Yisra'el**
    http://destination-yisrael.biblesearchers.com/destination-yis-rael/2012/04/the-jewish-cohens-practice-the-sacrifice-of-the-pe-sach-korban-lamb-has-the-day-of-the-messiah-come-.html

    Lamb selection by the Cohanim priest

14. **Jane the Actuary**
    http://www.patheos.com

    Awassi sheep - indigenous sheep of Bethlehem

15. **Sheep 101 – Lambing**
    http://www.sheep101.info

16. **International Christian Embassy Jerusalem (ICEJ)**
    http://www.int.icej.org

    Tower of the flock

17. **Creation.com**
    https://creation.com/darkness-at-the-crucifix-

ion-metaphor-or-real-history

The darkness during the crucifixion

18. **Astronomy Today**
   http://www.astronomytoday.com/- eclipses/ancient-part3.html

The darkness during the crucifixion

19. **National Catholic Register**
   https://www.ncregister.com/   -blog/what-does-science-say-about-the-darkness-during-the-crucifixion

The darkness during the crucifixion

20. **Oxford Bible Church**
   https://www.oxfordbiblechurch.co.uk/-index.php/teachings/end-time-prophecy/763-the-day-the-sun-stopped-shining

The darkness during the crucifixion

21. **Catholic Answers**
   https://www.catholic.com/

Adam and Eve, Original Sin, the Resurrection, and the definition of terms.

22. **Simply Catholic**
   https://www.simplycatholic.com/

Concupiscence and other definitions

ACKNOWLEDGEMENTS

I want to express my deepest and most heartfelt appreciation to my family, friends, and acquaintances who took the time out of their busy schedules to read the early draft of this work. Your feedback had a major impact on the modifications that were made to the original manuscript and your responses and comments were extremely valuable and greatly appreciated.

I want to extend a very special thank you to my wife Kathy Lastrapes. I want to thank my Pastor, Fr. Henry Sserriiso, Fr. Pat Kirsch and Fr. Sal Ragusa, for their positive and encouraging coments. Thank you to my son Martin Lastrapes who gave me the guidance that I needed in the development of this narrative. Additionally, I want thank my grandson Nathaniel Lastrapes, my daughter Reina Moore, my sister Myrtle Domingue and brother-in-law Preston Domingue. Thank you also to Tony Llorens for his very important inputs and his wife Jackie Llorens, Gina Madaio, Tom Imbruglia, Amanda Miller, Danny Centurioni, Bob Byrne, and Ryan Beck.

Made in the USA
Las Vegas, NV
09 July 2024